PIANO • VOCAL • GUITAR

CHRISTIAN MEMORIAL SONGS

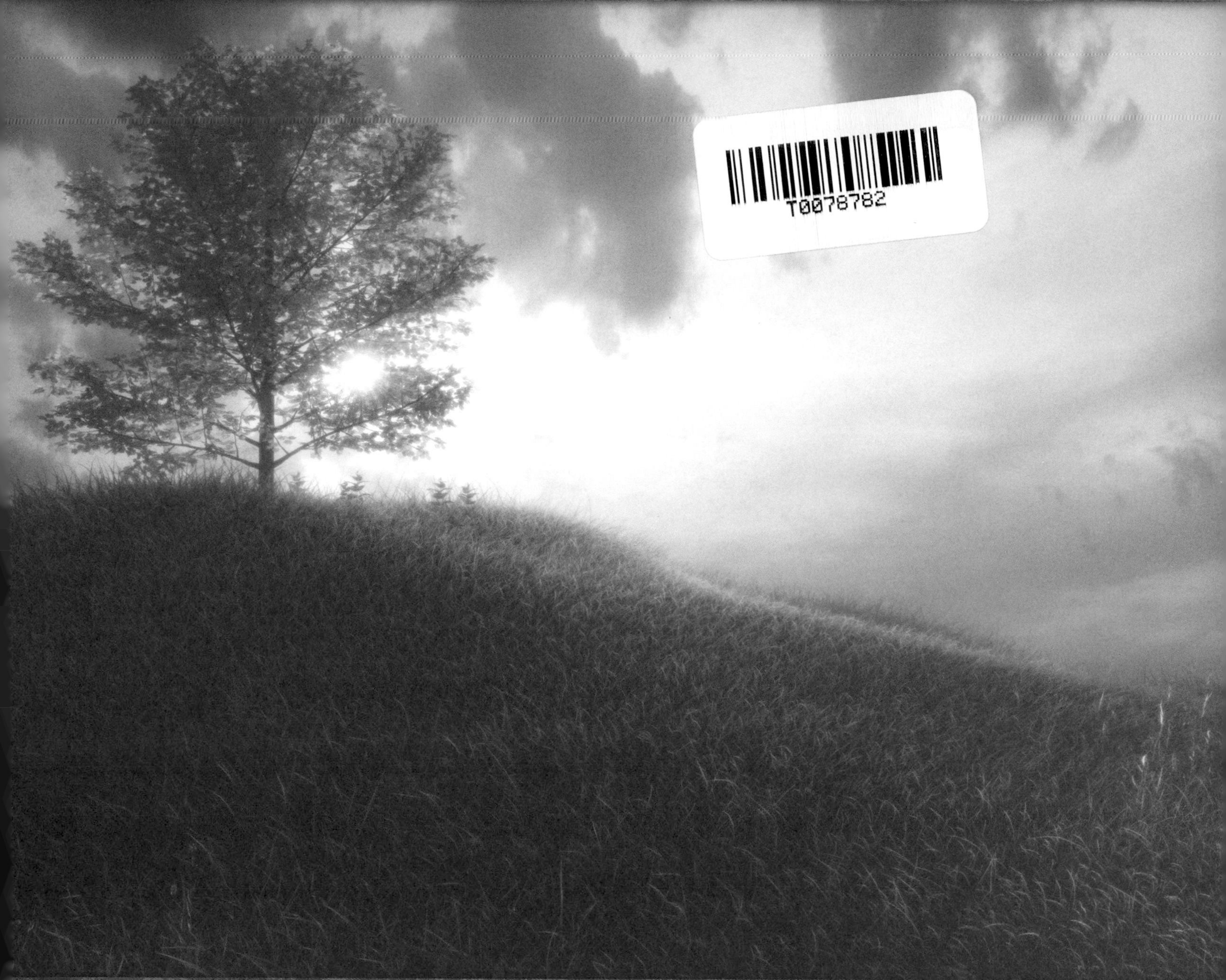

T0078782

ISBN 978-1-4234-7765-5

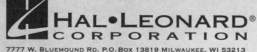

7777 W. BLUEMOUND RD. P.O. BOX 13819 MILWAUKEE, WI 53213

Visit Hal Leonard Online at
www.halleonard.com

AMAZING GRACE
(My Chains Are Gone)

Words by JOHN NEWTON
Traditional American Melody
Additional Words and Music by CHRIS TOMLIN
and LOUIE GIGLIO

Gently
G5
Gsus2
G5
3fr
mp
With pedal
Gsus2
G
Gsus
G
A - maz - ing grace, how sweet the sound that
D/G
G
Gsus2/B
saved a wretch like me. I once was lost but
Csus2
G
D/G
G
now I'm found, was blind but now I see. 'Twas

G
C(add2)/G
G
grace that taught my heart to fear, and grace my fears re-
Lord has prom-ised good to me, His Word my hope se-
D/G
G
G(add2)/B
C(add2)
G
lieved. How pre-cious did that grace ap-pear the
cures. He will my shield and por-tion be as
D/G
G
C/G
G
C
hour I first be-lieved.
long as life en-dures.
My chains are gone, I've been set
mf
G/B
C
free. My God, my Sav-ior has ran-somed

G/D
G/B
C
me. And like a flood, His mer - cy
G/B
D7sus/A
D7sus
1 G
rains un - end - ing love, a - maz - ing grace.
mp
D/G
G
D/G
The
2 G
G/B
C
G/B
grace. My chains are gone, I've been set free. My God, my
mf

C/E
G/D
Sav - ior has ran - somed me. And like a
C
G/B
flood, His mer - cy rains un - end - ing
D7sus/A
D7sus
G
C/G
G
love, a - maz - ing grace. The
mp
Gsus
3fr
G
earth shall soon dis - solve like snow, the sun for - bear to

D/G
G
Gsus2/B
Csus2
3fr
G
shine. But _ God, who _ called ___ me here be - low will

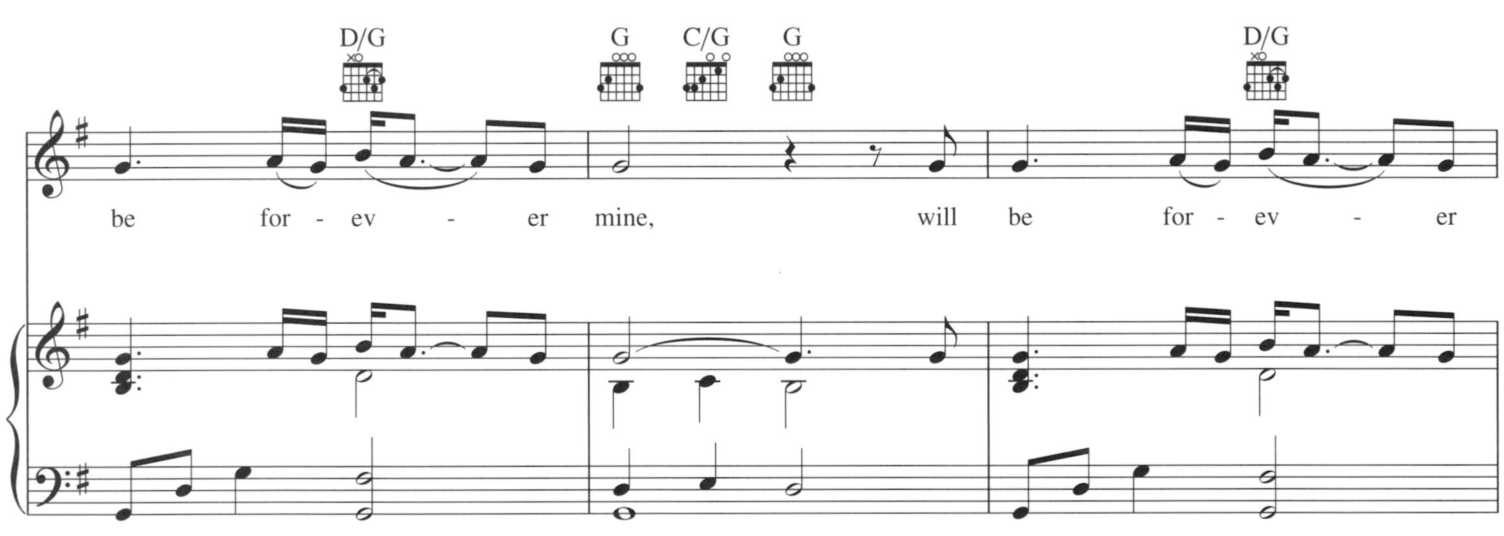
D/G
G
C/G
G
D/G
be for - ev - er mine, will be for - ev - er

G
C/G
G
D/G
G
mine. You are for - ev - er mine.
rit.

BLESSED BE YOUR NAME

Words and Music by MATT REDMAN
and BETH REDMAN

* *Recorded a half step lower.*

G6
be Your name.
be Your name.
D
A
Bless - ed be Your name when I'm
Bless - ed be Your name on the
Bm7
G
found in the des - ert place, though I
road marked with suf - fer - ing, though there's
D
A
walk through the wil - der - ness, bless - ed
pain in the of - fer - ing, bless - ed

G(add2)
D
be Your name.
be Your name.
Ev - 'ry bless - ing
A
Bm7
G
You pour out I'll turn back to praise.
D
A
Bm7
When the dark - ness clos - es in, Lord,
still I will
G
D
A
say: Bless - ed be the name of the Lord,
bless - ed be Your

Bm7
G
D
name.
Bless - ed be the name of the Lord,
Asus
Bm7
1 G
blessed - ed be Your glo - ri - ous name.
2 G(add2)
D
A
You give and take a - way, You
Bm7
G
D
give and take a - way.
My heart will choose to

A
Bm7
G
say, "Lord, bless - ed be Your name."
D
A
Ev - 'ry bless - ing You pour out I'll
Bm7
G
D
turn back to praise.
When the dark - ness
A
Bm7
G
clos - es in, Lord,
still I'm gon - na say:
Bless - ed be the

D A Bm7
name of the Lord, bless - ed be Your name, Je -
G D A
sus. Bless - ed be the name of the Lord, bless - ed be Your
Bm7 G D
glo - ri - ous name. Bless - ed be the name of the Lord,
A Bm7 G
bless - ed be Your name. Bless - ed be the

D
Asus
Bm7
name of the Lord, blessed be Your glo - ri - ous name.
G
D
A
You give and take a - way, You
Bm7
G
D
give and take a - way. My heart will choose to
A
Bm7
G
D(add2)
say, "Lord, bless - ed be Your name." Yeah, yeah.

DANCING WITH THE ANGELS

Words and Music by ED CASH,
TRENT MONK and MICHAEL NEAGLE

In a slow 2
D
Dmaj7
D/C♯
Dmaj7/C♯
Gmaj9/B
2fr
mp
Gmaj7
G6
D
D/C♯
Mem-'ries sur-round_ me, but sad-ness has found_ me. I'd
G(add2)/B
G
D
do an-y-thing_ for more time._ Nev-er be-fore_ has
D/C♯
G(add2)/B
G
some-one meant more, and I can't get you out_ of my mind.

Bm
A
G
Gsus2
There is so much that I don't un - der - stand, but I know
mf
A7sus
D
D/C♯
Bm7
D/A
you're danc-ing with the an - gels, walk-ing in new
f
Gsus2
D/F♯
Em7(add4)
5fr
A7sus
life. Danc - ing with the an -
D
D/C♯
Bm7
D/A
Gsus2
D/F♯
To Coda
- gels. Heav-en fills your eyes

Em7(add4)
5fr
A7sus
G
Bm7
now that you're danc - ing with the an - gels.
A
Gsus2
Gsus2/B
A
mf
You had
D
D/C♯
G(add2)/B
love for your fam - 'ly, love for all peo - ple, love for the Fa - ther and Son.
G
D
Your heart will be heard in your

A/C♯
Bm
G
D.S. al Coda
un - spo - ken words
through
gen - er - a - tions to come.
CODA
Em7(add4)
A7sus
Bm
now that you're danc - ing.
We're on - ly here
for such a short time.
C(add2)
I'm gon - na
G6
A
stand up, shout out, and sing, "Hal - le - lu - jah!"
And one day I'll see you a - gain,

D
D/C♯
Bm7
D/A
and we'll be danc - ing with the an - gels,
walk-ing in new
Gsus2
D/F♯
Em7(add4)
5fr
A7sus
D
D/C♯
life.
Danc-ing with the an - gels.
Bm7
D/A
Gsus2
D/F♯
Em7(add4)
5fr
A7sus
Heav-en will fill our eyes
when we're danc - ing with the an -
D
D/C♯
Bm7
D/A
Gsus2
D/F♯
- gels,

Em7(add4)
A7sus
D
D/C♯
Bm7
D/A
when we're danc - ing with the an - gels.
Gsus2
D/F♯
Em7(add4)
A7sus
D
D/C♯
Danc - ing with the an - gels.
mf
Bm7
D/A
Gsus2
D/F♯
Em7(add4)
A7sus
Danc - ing with the an -
D
D/C♯
Bm7
D/A
G
A7
D
- gels.
rit.
mp

EVERY SINGLE TEAR

Words and Music by SCOTT KRIPPAYNE
and STEVE SILER

* *Recorded a half step higher.*

Dm11
3fr
C/E
there's some-bod - y watch - ing o - ver you, and
When you're like a heart with - out a home,
F(add2)
Dm7/G
He knows ev - 'ry - thing you're go - ing through.
you don't have to face this hurt a - lone, 'cause
He sees
F
C/E
3
ev - 'ry sin - gle tear, He feels ev - 'ry - thing you're feel - ing. He
(D.S. a tempo)
Dm11
G7sus
C
Gm11
C7
wants to hold you close and dry your eyes. Oh, your

To Coda
Fmaj9
Em7
Am11
3fr
heart is what He hears when the world just hears you cry - ing. No
Dm11
3fr
Dm7/G
mat - ter what the pain, He cares a - bout ev - 'ry sin - gle
1
F
Am11
3fr
tear.
Fmaj7
Dm11
3fr
C/E
F/A
B♭sus2
F/A
O - ver - whelmed by cir - cum-stanc - es

2
C
G/A
3fr
Am
tear. If God a - dorns the lil - ies of the field
F
Dm11
3fr
Dm7/G
and cares for ev - 'ry spar - row in the
C
G/B
B♭sus2
F/A
sky, how much more is He a - ware of your sor -
Fm/A♭
C/G
Dm11
3fr
- row and de - spair? How much does He care a - bout your
poco rall.

D.S. al Coda
Fm6
F/G
C/E
CODA
Em7
Am11
G
3fr
life? He sees
just hears you cry - ing. No
F(add2)
Dm11
Dm7/G
C/E
mat - ter what the pain, He cares a - bout ev - 'ry sin - gle
F
C/E
tear. He feels ev - 'ry - thing you're feel - ing. He
Dm11
G7sus
G7
C
Gm7
G♭7♭5
wants to hold you close and dry your eyes. Oh, your

Fmaj9
Em7
Am
G
Em7
heart is what He hears when the world just hears you cry - ing. No
Dm11
3fr
Fm6/A♭
6fr
Fm6/G
Fm6
mat - ter what the pain, He cares
G7sus
F
a - bout ev - 'ry sin - gle tear.
Am9
5fr
G
F
G(add4)
C(add9)
rall.

FINALLY HOME

Words and Music by BART MILLARD,
BARRY GRAUL and MIKE SCHEUCHZER

Gently
A
mp
E
1
2
C♯m
4fr
Gon-na wrap my arms a - round my dad - dy's neck
A
E
and tell him that I've missed him.

C♯m
4fr
And tell him all a - bout the man that I be - came,
A
and hope that it pleased him.
E
B
There's so much I wan - na say, so much
A
I want - ed you to know.
E

A
Asus2(♯4)
When I fi - n'lly
A
A6
E
make it home.
A
Asus2(♯4)
When I fi - n'lly
A
A6
E
To Coda
make it home.

C♯m
4fr
Then I'll gaze up - on the throne of the King,
A
E
fro - zen in my steps.
C♯m
4fr
And all the ques - tions that I swore I would ask,
A
E
words just won't come yet.

B
I'm so a - mazed at what I've seen, so much more
A
E
than this old mind can hold.
D.S. al Coda
When I
CODA
And the sweet-
B
A
- est sound these ears have yet to hear: the voic - es of the an - gels.

E
Esus(add2)
F♯m/E
E
B
Ah.
A
E
When I fi - n'lly
A
Asus2(♯4)
A
A6
E
make it home.

A
Asus2(♯4)
When I fi - n'lly
A
A6
E
make it home.
A6
Ooh.
Amaj7
E

HE WILL CARRY YOU

Words and Music by
SCOTT WESLEY BROWN

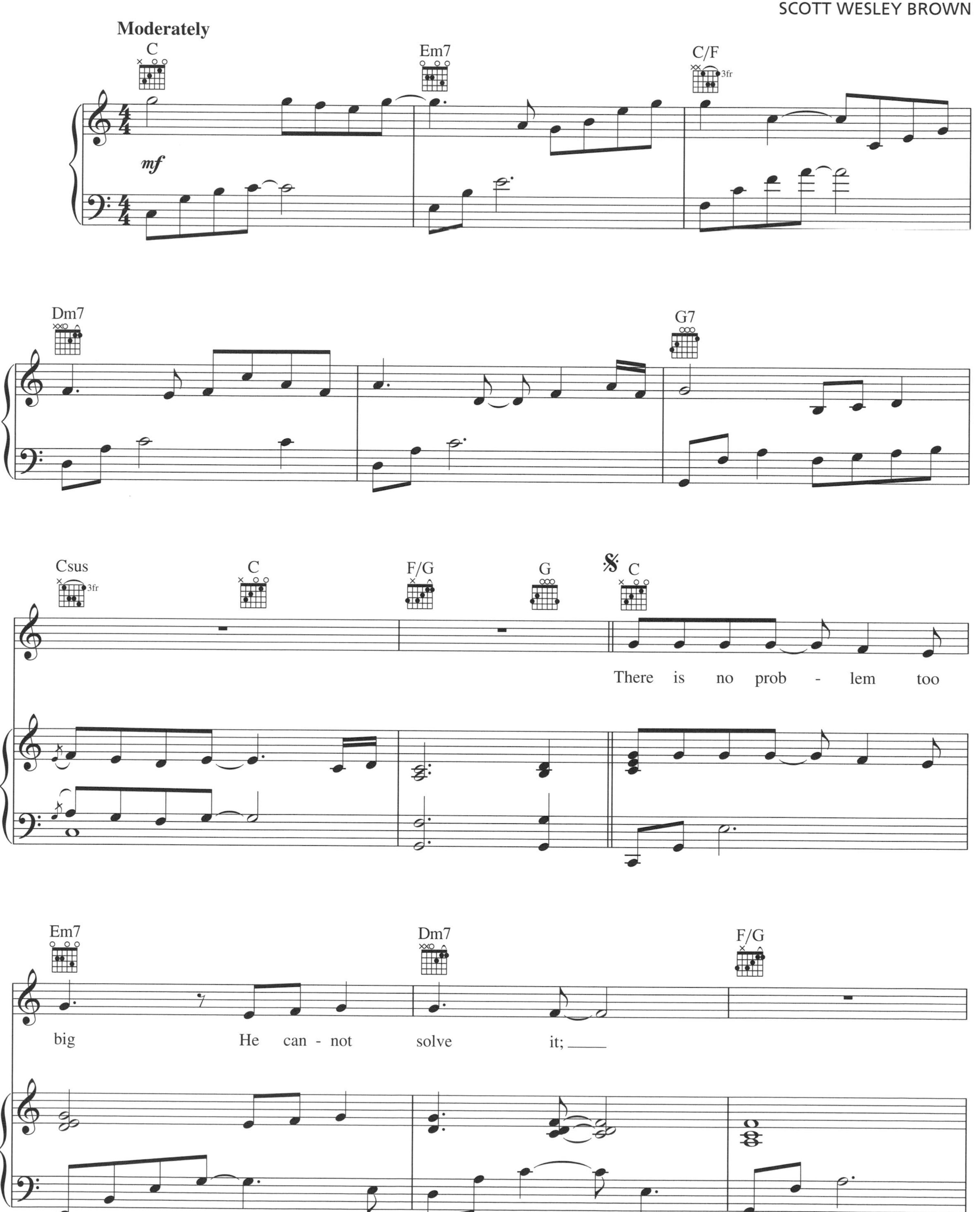
Moderately
C
Em7
C/F
3fr
mf
Dm7
G7
Csus
3fr
C
F/G
G
C
There is no prob - lem too
Em7
Dm7
F/G
big He can - not solve it;

Dm7
G7
Dm/C
C
there is no moun - tain too tall He can - not move it.
F/G
G
C
Em7
There is no storm too dark God can - not
Dm7
F/G
Dm7
calm it; there is no sor - row too
G7
Dm/C
C
F/G
G
deep He can - not soothe it. If He

Half-time feel
C
Cmaj7
carried the weight of the world upon His shoulders,
Dm7
F/G
Dm7
I know, my {brother, sister,} that He
F/G
G7
To Coda
1, 3
C
F/C
C
F/G
G
will carry you.
If He
2
C
F/C
C
F/G
G
Am
you.
He said, "Come unto

Em7
G
D
Me, all who are wea - ry,
Dsus
D
F
G
and I will give you
D.S. al Coda
(with repeat)
Csus
3fr
C
F/G
G
rest."
CODA
C
F/C
C
A7sus
you. If He

D
Dmaj7
Em7/D
car-ried the weight of the world up-on His shoul - ders,
A7sus/D
A7/D
Em7
G/A
A7
I know, my broth - er, sis - ter, that He will car - ry
D
G/A
A7
G/A
1
2
2fr
3fr
you.
If He
He will car - ry
G/D
A
D
you.
He will car - ry you.

GIVE ME JESUS

Words and Music by
JEREMY CAMP

Em7
Am
F
Je - sus, give me Je - sus.
C
Am
F
You can have all this world, just give me Je -
To Coda
C
Am
- sus. When I am a - lone,
F
C
Am
when I am a - lone, oh, when I am a - lone,

F
C
D.S. al Coda
give me Je - sus. Give me
CODA
C
Am7
sus.
mf
F(add2)
Csus(add2)
C
Je - sus. Give me
Am7
F(add2)
C
Je - sus.

Am
F
When I come to die, when I come to die,
mp
C
Am
F
oh, when I come to die, give me Je -
C
Em7
sus. Give me Je - sus,
Am7
Fmaj7
C
give me Je - sus. You can have

Am7
F
all this world, just give me Je -
C
Em7
Am7
C/G
sus. Give me Je - sus, give me
mf
Fmaj7
C
Am7
Je - sus. You can have all this
F
Am7
F
world, you can have all this world, you can have

Am7
F
F(add2)
all this world,
just give me Je -
mp
C(add2)
Am7
- sus.
(Vocal 1st time only)
mf
F(add2)
Csus(add2)
C
C(add2)
Je - sus.
Am7
F(add2)
C

HOMESICK

Words and Music by
BART MILLARD

Moderately, with feeling
Fsus2
F
B♭
B♭6
Csus
3fr
F/C
mf
B♭/D
B♭maj7
Fsus2
F6/9
C7/F
You're
Fsus2
B♭sus2
in a bet - ter place, I've heard a thou - sand times. And at
Help me, Lord, 'cause I don't un - der - stand Your ways. The
Fsus2
B♭sus2
least a thou - sand times I've re - joiced for you. But the
rea - son why, I won - der if I'll ev - er know. But

E♭
C
F/A
reason why I'm broken, the reason why I cry is how
even if You showed me, the hurt would be the same 'cause I'm
B♭sus2
F
Fsus
long must I wait to be with you?
still here so far away from home.
F
B♭sus2
C5
I close my eyes and I see Your face. If home's where my heart is, then I'm
F
C/E
Dm
C
out of place. Lord, won't You give me strength to make it through somehow.

B♭sus2
Csus
3fr
B♭sus2
1
F
I've nev-er been more home - sick than now.
B♭sus2
Csus
3fr
B♭sus2
2
F
Fsus
F
C
In Christ there are no good - byes.
B♭sus2
C
B♭sus2
And in Christ there is no end.
So I'll

C
Dm
hold on to Je - sus with all that I have to see
Gm
3fr
C5
3fr
F
you a - gain, to see you a - gain. And I close my eyes and I
B♭sus2
Dm
F/A
B♭sus2
see Your face. If home's where my heart is, then I'm out of place. Lord, won't You
Csus
3fr
B♭sus2/D
give me strength to make it through some - how. Won't You

C/E
C5
3fr
B♭sus2
give me strength to make it through some - how.
Won't You give
Csus
3fr
B♭sus2/D
me strength to make it through some - how.
I've
C5
3fr
B♭sus2
F
nev-er been more home - sick
than now.
B♭sus2
Csus
3fr
B♭sus2

IN CHRIST ALONE

Words and Music by KEITH GETTY
and STUART TOWNEND

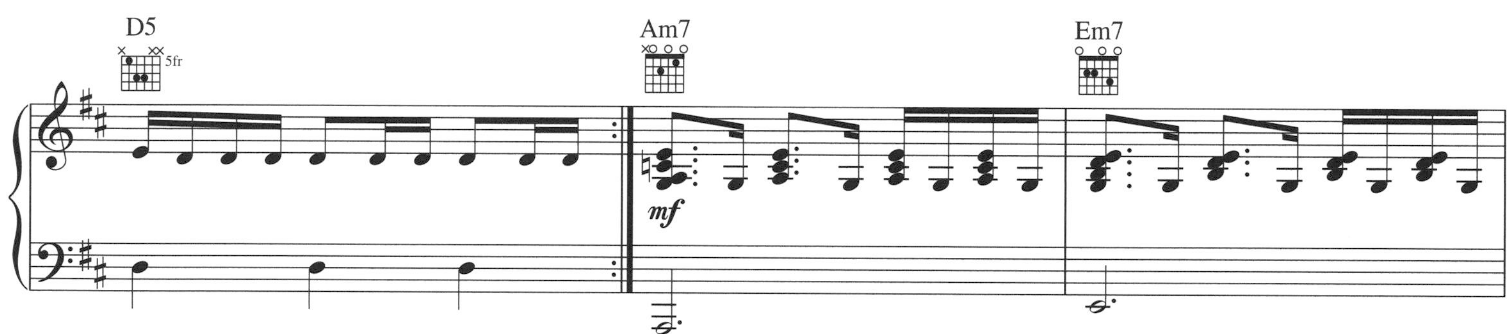

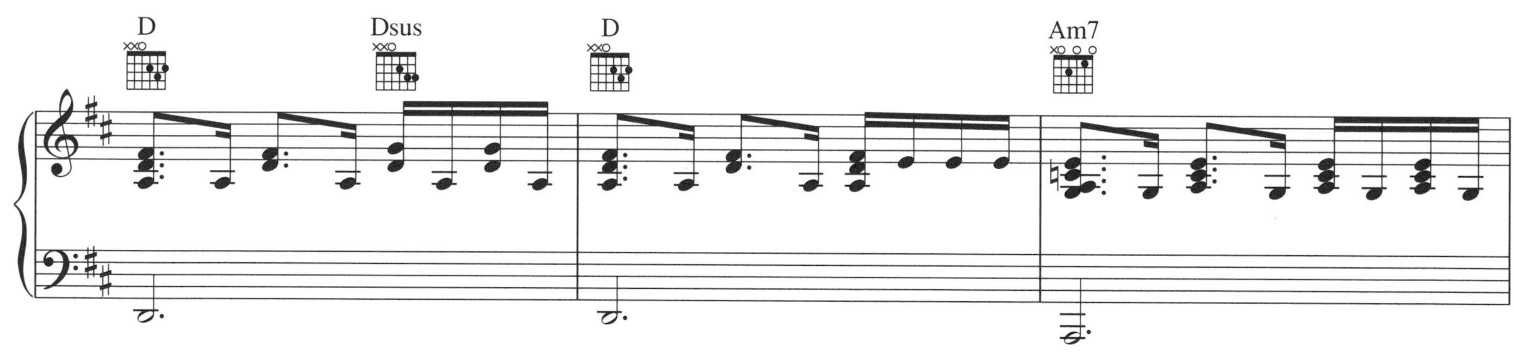

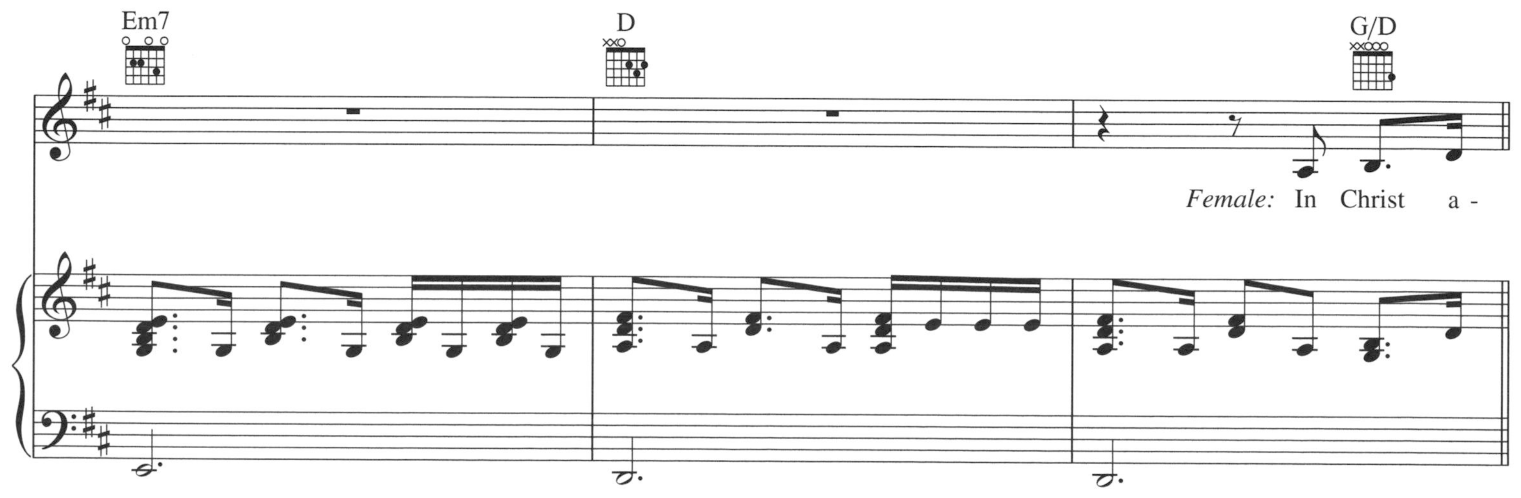

D
A
D/F♯
G
D/F♯
Em
G/A
3fr
lone my hope is found; He is my light, my strength, my
lone, who took on flesh, full - ness of God in help - less
D
G
D
G
A
D/F♯
song. This cor - ner - stone, this sol - id ground, firm through the
Babe! This gift of love and right - eous - ness, scorned by the
G
D/F♯
Em
G/A
3fr
D
D/F♯
fierc - est drought and storm. What heights of
ones He came to save. 'Til on that
G
D/F♯
Asus
A
D/F♯
G
Bm7
love, what depths of peace, when fears are stilled, when striv - ings
cross as Je - sus died, the wrath of God was sat - is -

Asus
A
G
D
G
A
D/F♯
cease. My com - fort - er, my all in all, here in the
fied, for ev - 'ry sin on Him was laid; here in the
G
D/F♯
Em
G/A
1
D
G
love of Christ I stand. In Christ a -
death of Christ I
2
D
Am7
Em7
live. (Oh.
D
Am7
Oh.)

Em7 D G/D
There in the
D A/D G/D Em/D
ground His bod - y lay, Light of the world by dark - ness
D G D G A D/F♯
slain. Then, burst - ing forth in glo - rious day, up from the
G D/F♯ Em G/A D G D/F♯
grave He rose a - gain! And as He stands in vic - to -
3fr
cresc.
f

Asus
A
D/F♯
G
Bm7
Asus
A
G
ry, sin's curse has lost its grip on me. For I am
D
G
A
D/F♯
G
D/F♯
Em
G/A
3fr
His and He is mine, bought with the pre - cious blood of
D
Am7
Em7
Christ. (Oh, oh.)
dim.
D
G/D
D
No guilt in life, no fear in
mp

A
D/F♯
G
D/F♯
Em
A
D
G
death; this is the pow'r of Christ in me. From life's first
D
A
D/F♯
G
D/F♯
Em
Asus
cry to fi - nal breath, Je - sus com - mands my des - ti - ny.
cresc.
D
D/F♯
G
D/F♯
Asus
A
D/F♯
No pow'r of hell, no scheme of man, can ev - er
Lead vocal ad lib.
f
G
Bm7
Asus
A
G
D
G
pluck me from His hand. 'Til He re - turns or calls me

A
D/F♯
G
D/F♯
Em
G/A
D
3fr
home, here in the pow'r of Christ I'll stand.
Am7
Em7
D
(Oh, oh.
Am7
Em7
Oh, oh.)
D
G/A
D
G/A
D
dim. to end

I WILL RISE

Words and Music by CHRIS TOMLIN,
JESSE REEVES, LOUIE GIGLIO
and MATT MAHER

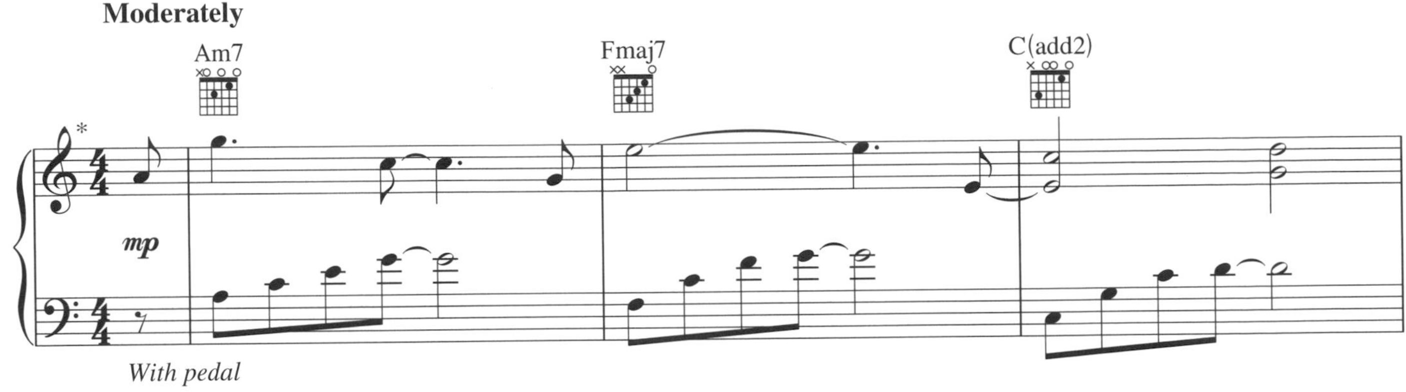
Moderately
Am7
Fmaj7
C(add2)
mp
With pedal

G5
3fr
Am7
F
There's a peace I've come to know, though my

C
G
Am7
heart and flesh may fail. There's an an - chor for my soul.

* *Recorded a half step lower.*

F
C
G
I can say, "It is well." Je-
C
G/C
Am7
-sus has o - ver - come, and the grave is o - ver - whelmed.
F
C/E
Gsus
3fr
G
The vic - to - ry is won; He is
Am7
F
C
ris - en from the dead. And I will rise when He calls

G
Am7
F
my name; no more sor - row, no more pain. I will rise
C
G
Am7
on ea - gles' wings, be - fore my God fall on
F
C/E
F
my knees, and rise. I will rise.
C/G
G
Am7
There's a day that's draw - ing near

F
C
G
when this dark - ness breaks to light, and the
Am7
F
C
shad - ows dis - ap - pear, and my faith shall be my eyes.
G
C
G/B
Je - sus has o - ver - come, and the grave
Am7
F
C/E
is o - ver - whelmed. The vic - to - ry is won;

G/B
Am7
G
F
He is ris - en from the dead. And I will rise
cresc.
C
G
Am7
when He calls my name; no more sor - row, no
mf
F
C
G
more pain. I will rise on ea - gles' wings, be - fore
Am7
F
C/E
my God fall on my knees, and rise.

F
C/G
G
I will rise.
cresc.
F
C
G
And I hear the voice of man - y an - gels sing, "Wor -
f
F
G
F
C
- thy is the Lamb!" And I hear the cry of ev - 'ry long -
1
G
F
C
G
- ing heart, "Wor - thy is the Lamb!" And I hear the voice

2
G
Am7
F
C
- ing heart, "Wor - thy is the Lamb!
G
F
C
G
Wor - thy is the Lamb!"
C
G/C
Am
mp
F
C
G
I will rise when He calls my name; no

Am7
F
C
more sor - row, no more pain. I will rise on ea -
G
Am7
F
- gles' wings, be - fore my God fall on my knees, and rise.
C/E
F
C/G
I will rise.
F/A
C/G
G
C
I will rise.
rit.

IF YOU COULD SEE ME NOW

Words and Music by
KIM NOBLITT

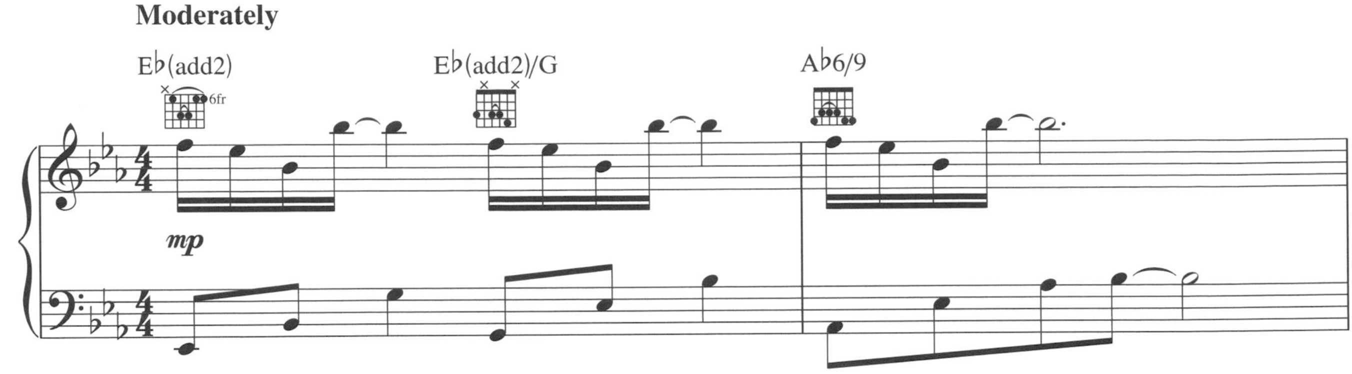
Moderately
Eb(add2)
6fr
Eb(add2)/G
Ab6/9
mp

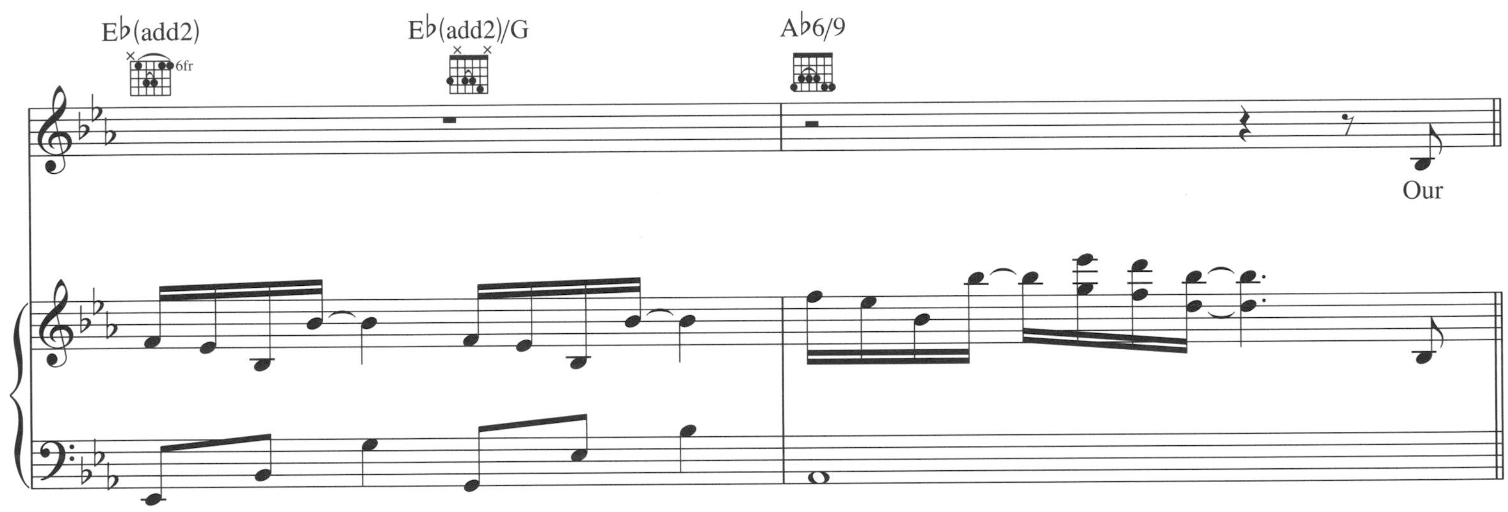
Eb(add2)
6fr
Eb(add2)/G
Ab6/9
Our

Eb
3fr
Ab(add2)/Eb
prayers have all been an - swered; I fi - nal - ly ar - rived. The
light and tem - po - rar - y trials have worked out for my good, to

Fm7
Ab/Bb
Bb/D
Eb
Ab/Bb
heal - ing that had been de - layed has now been re - al - ized.
know it brought Him glo - ry when I mis - un - der - stood.
Eb
Bb7sus/F
Eb/G
Ab
Fm7
No one's in a hur - ry; there's no sched - ule to keep. We're
Tho' we've had our sor - rows, they can nev - er com - pare. What
Cm7
F13
F7
Fm7
Abmaj7
all en - joy - ing Je - sus, just sit - ting at His
Je - sus has in store for us, no lan - guage can
Bb9sus
Bb7b9
Eb
Ebsus2/G
feet.
share. If you could see me now, I'm
mf

A♭(add2)
B♭7sus
B♭7
E♭
Gm7
walk - ing streets of gold. If you could see me now, I'm
A♭(add2)
B♭7sus
G/B
Cm7
Gm/B♭
stand - ing tall and whole. If you could see me now, you'd
Fm7
A♭maj9
B♭
G/B
Cm7
Gm/B♭
know I've seen His face. If you could see me now, you'd
1
Fm7
A♭maj9
Fm7/B♭
Fm7
know the pain's e - rased. You would-n't want me to ev - er
mp

Fm7/B♭
Fm7
leave this place
if you could on - ly see
me now. My
2
Fm7
A♭maj9
B♭7sus
B♭7
know the pain's e - rased.
Gm
C/F
E♭maj9
Csus2/E
B♭/C
C/E
F
F(add2)/A
If you could see me now, I'm
B♭(add2)
B♭(add2)/C
F
Am7
walk - ing streets of gold. If you could see me now, I'm

B♭(add2) B♭(add2)/C A/C♯ Dm Am/C
3fr 3fr
stand - ing tall and whole. If you could see me now, you'd
Gm7 B♭maj9 C A/C♯ Dm Am/C
5fr
know I've seen His face. If you could see me now, you'd
Gm7 B♭maj9 Gm7/C Gm7
5fr
know the pain's e - rased. You would-n't want me to ev - er
mp sub.
Gm7/C Gm7
leave this per - fect place if you could on - ly see me

Gm7/C
F(add2)
now, if you could see ___ me now,
rit.
freely

Fsus
F
F/A
if you could on - ly see me ___ now. ___

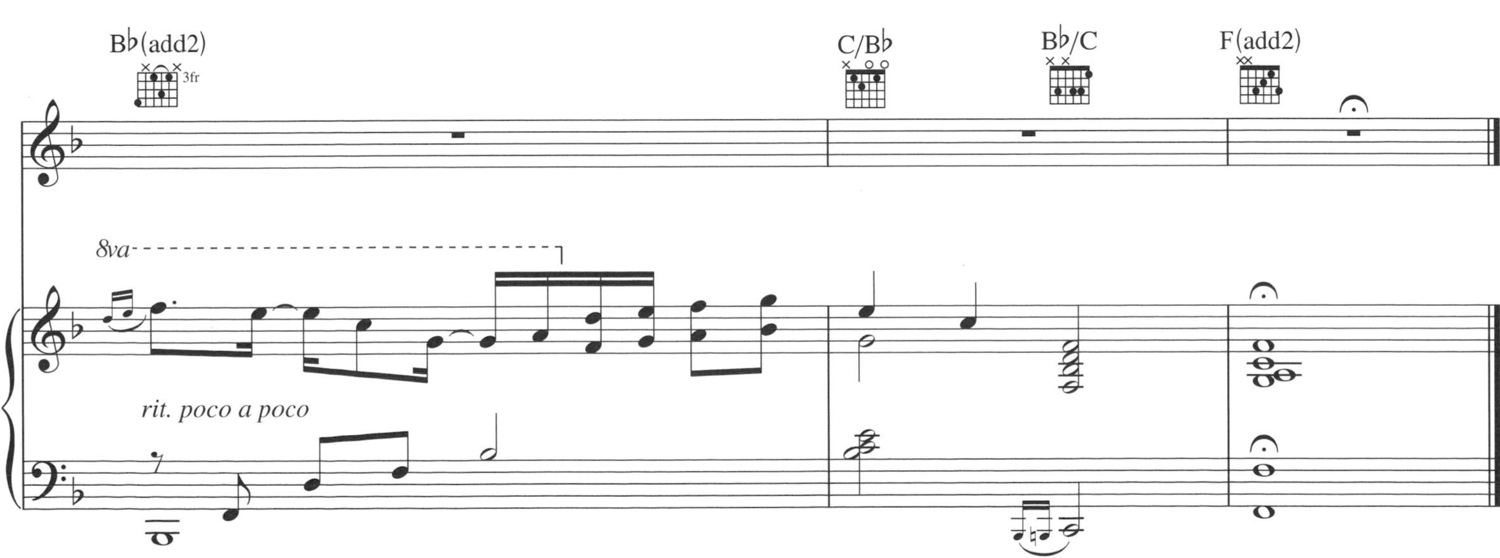
B♭(add2)
3fr
C/B♭
B♭/C
F(add2)
8va
rit. poco a poco

IN HIS PRESENCE

Words and Music by DICK TUNNEY
and MELODIE TUNNEY

With expression
Cbmaj7
Abm7
Abm6/Eb
Ebm7
mp
Abm
Gb/Bb
Cbmaj7
Dbsus
Db
Eb(add2)
Bb/Ab
Ab
Eb/G
In the qui - et of this hour, as I
be such sweet re - ward when we
rit.
a tempo
Bb/Ab
Ab/Bb
Eb
Bb/D
Cm
Cm/Bb
kneel be - fore You now, I be - lieve Your
wait up - on the Lord! As we take the time, He
8va

F7/A
Ab/Bb
Bb
Abmaj7/Bb
Bb
Eb/G
promise to be faithful. I don't
gives His perfect wisdom, to be
Bb/Ab
Ab
Eb/G
Bb/Ab
Ab/Bb
Bdim7
always understand what Your perfect will de-
found in Him alone. All our deepest secrets
Cm
Cm/Bb
Ab6
Eb/G
mands, but I've learned to trust You more in Your
known, we're surrounded by His grace when we
cresc.
To Coda
Dbmaj7
Ab/Bb
Bb
Ab/Eb
Eb
presence, Lord. In Your presence
seek His face.
mf

Eb/G
Bb/Ab
Ab
C/G
there is com - fort,
in Your
Fsus(add2)
Fm
Fm/Eb
Db
Ab/C
pres - ence
there is peace.
Bb
Bb/Ab
Eb/G
Ab
When we seek to know Your heart, we will
Eb/Bb
Cm
Fm7
find such blessed as - sur - ance in Your ho - ly

A♭maj7/B♭
B♭9
E♭(add2)
6fr
D.S. al Coda
pres - ence, Lord.
There can
mp
CODA
A♭/B♭
4fr
B♭/C
B♭/F
F
F/A
In Your pres - ence there is
f
C/B♭
B♭
D/A
Gsus(add2)
Gm
3fr
com - fort, in Your pres - ence
Gm/F
E♭
3fr
B♭/D
B♭/C
C/B♭
there is peace. When we

F/A
B♭(add2)
3fr
F/C
Dm7
seek the Fa - ther's heart, we will find such blessed as - sur - ance. An
mp
Gm7
F/A
B♭
F/A
ev - er - o - pen door to know our Sav - ior more, in the
Gm
3fr
B♭/C
C
F(add2)
Dm
pres - ence of our Lord.
Gm7
F/A
Gm/B♭
C
D(add2)
mf
pp

NO MORE NIGHT

Words and Music by
WALT HARRAH

C♭maj7
A♭m7
E♭
Gone is the curse from which I stum - bled and fell.
Slow - ly the names from the book are read.
C♭maj9
A♭m11
B♭7sus
E - vil is ban - ished to e - ter - nal hell.
I know the King so there's no need, no need to dread.
E♭(add2)
Cm7
B♭7/D
No more night. No more
E♭
B♭sus2/D
Cm
Fm11
Fm7/B♭
pain. No more tears. Nev - er cry - ing a -

B♭/A♭
E♭/G
A♭(add2)
F/A
B♭
G/B
gain. And prais - es to the great "I AM." We will
Cm
Fm11
Fm7/B♭
B♭
1
E♭
Cm7/E♭
live in the light of the ris - en Lamb.
Emaj9
C♯m6
E♭(add2)/B♭
B♭7sus
See all a -
mf
2
E♭
D♭
B♭/D
A♭/E♭
Lamb. See o - ver there, there's a man - sion, oh, that's pre - pared just for

E♭/G
Fm7
E♭
D♭
B♭(add2)/D
A♭(add2)/C
B♭
Csus
me, where I will live with my Sav - ior e - ter - nal -
C
B♭(add2)/D
B♭maj9
Csus
N.C.
ly. And there will be no more night.
Slower
F(add2)
Gm7(add4)
C7/E
F
C/E
Dm7
Gm7
No more night. No more pain. No more tears. Nev - er
B♭
Csus
C/B♭
F(add2)/A
B♭(add2)
G(add2)/B
Csus
C
A7
cry - ing a - gain. Prais - es to the great "I AM." We will

Dm
Gm7
B♭maj7
C
F
F/C
C
F(add2)/A
B♭
live in the light of the ris - en Lamb. Oh, praises to the
G(add2)/B
Csus
C
Dm
Gm7
B♭maj9
C
C/E
great "I AM." We will live in the light of the ris - en, the ris - en
N.C.
F
Gm7
C(add2)/E
B♭(add2)/D
B♭sus2
Lamb.
Fm7
E♭sus2
F
rit.
a tempo

IT IS WELL

Traditional
Arranged by DAVE LEUTKENHOELTER

Cm
B♭sus
sor - rows like sea bil - lows roll;
B♭
E♭
E♭/G
what - ev - er my lot, Thou has
A♭
B♭
Cm
taught me to say, "It is well, it is
B♭
E♭
well with my soul." It is
f

B♭/D
E♭
3fr
B♭/D
E♭
3fr
A♭
4fr
well
with
my
soul,
Fm7
E♭/G
3fr
Cm
3fr
E♭
3fr
it
is
well
with
my
A♭
4fr
Cm
3fr
soul.
My
sin,
O
the
mf
A♭
4fr
bliss
of
this
glo
-
ri
-
ous
thought:
my

Cm
3fr
B♭sus
sin, not in part, but the whole
Cm
3fr
is nailed to the cross and I
A♭
4fr
Cm
3fr
bear it no more. Praise the Lord, praise the
B♭sus
Lord, O my soul! It is
cresc.

E♭
3fr
well
with
my
soul,
f
Cm
3fr
B♭sus
A♭
4fr
it
is
well
with
my
E♭
3fr
soul.
It
is
well
with
my
soul,
it
is

Cm
3fr
B♭
A♭
4fr
E♭
3fr
well with my soul.
mp
And, Lord, haste the day when my
faith shall be sight, the clouds be rolled
back as a scroll. The

trump shall re - sound and the Lord shall de -
scend; "e - ven so," it is well with my
soul. It is
well with my soul,
Cm
Cm/D
Cm/E♭
E♭
3fr
f sub.

1
2
Cm
B♭sus
A♭
E♭
3fr
4fr
it is well
with my
soul.
It is
with my
soul.
mp

NO MORE PAIN

Words and Music by GEOFF THURMAN,
BECKY THURMAN and MICHAEL ENGLISH

Moderately slow
A
D/F♯
E7/G♯
D/A
A
mp
F♯m7
G(add2)
Dsus2
She
E/G♯
A
E/G♯
F♯m7
sits by the win - dow with wan - der - ing eyes. She has a
G(add2)
Dsus2
E
A
3
song in her heart and a gold - en dis - guise. Her

E/G♯
A
E/G♯
F♯m7
bod - y is torn be - cause age does - n't heal. She's
G(add2)
Dsus2
E
A
Bm
not let - ting on a - bout the pain that she feels. But she
C
Am7
Fmaj7
C/E
knows in her soul that it won't be too long 'til
E♭
Cm7
3fr
3fr
A♭maj7
B♭
Je - sus comes back to car - ry her home, where there will be

E♭
A♭/C
B♭/D
E♭sus(add2)
E♭
Cm7
D♭(add2)
no more pain, no more sor - row, no more wait - ing for il -
A♭
E♭/B♭
B♭
E♭
A♭/C
B♭/D
A♭m6/E♭
E♭
lu - sive to - mor - rows. There will be no more pain, no more dy - ing,
Cm7
D♭
Cm7
A♭(add2)
E♭/B♭
B♭
A♭sus2
no more striv - ing or strain, no more pain.
E/G♯
A
My mind's eye re - mem - bers the

E/G♯
F♯m7
G(add2)
Dsus2
trou - ble I've seen, all I have been through, and how I
E
A
E/G♯
A
E/G♯
F♯m7
long to be free. But I learn by her pa - tience that I need her re - solve to
G(add2)
Dsus2
E
A
Bm
wait for the o - p'ning of e - ter - ni - ty's halls. And I
mf
C
Am7
Fmaj7
C/E
know that in time we will stand side by side, when

Eb
Cm7
Abmaj7
Bb
Jesus comes back receiving His bride, where there will be
Eb
Ab/C
Bb/D
Fm/Eb
Db(add2)
no more pain, no more sorrow, no more waiting for illusive tomorrows.
Ab
Eb/Bb
Abm6/Eb
There will be no more pain, no more dying,
Db
Ab(add2)
no more striving or strain, no more. No more pain,
f
cues: optional

B♭/D
Fm/E♭
E♭
3fr
E
Dmaj7
no more sor - row, no more wait - ing for il -
A
E/G♯
F♯m7
A/B
E
A/C♯
lu - sive to - mor - rows. There will be no more pain,
cresc.
f
B/D♯
4fr
Am6/E
E
C♯m7
D
A(add2)
E/B
B
no more dy - ing, no more striv - ing or strain, no more.
F♯m/E
D(add2)
No more pain, no more sor - row, no more wait - ing for il -

A
E/B
B
E
A/C♯
B/D♯
4fr
Am6/E
E
lu - sive to - mor - rows. No more pain, no more dy - ing,
C♯m7
4fr
D
C♯m7
4fr
A(add2)
E/B
B
Asus2
no more striv - ing or strain, no more pain.
E/A
No more pain.
mp
No more pain.
Repeat and Fade
Optional Ending
Asus2
E
rit.

ON THE OTHER SIDE

Words and Music by KEVIN DENNEY,
JIMMY FORTUNE and TOM BOTKIN

A♭
4fr
E♭
3fr
no such thing as time.
Where the streets are paved with gold
B♭
and you nev - er grow old on the
E♭
3fr
B♭7sus
oth - er side.
B♭7
E♭
3fr
On the oth - er side
oth - er side do you

B♭
E♭
3fr
ev - 'ry - bod - y sings.
ev - er see me cry?
There's miles and miles of flow -
Do you know how much I miss
A♭
4fr
- ers and lots of pret - ty things.
you? Wish I could have said good - bye.
Where the
Just
E♭
3fr
B♭7
sky is a per - fect blue
one more "I love you."
and ev - 'ry - thing looks brand - new
Oh, am I real - ly get - ting through
E♭
3fr
on the oth - er side.
on the oth - er side?

Fm
E♭/G
A♭
3fr
4fr
Well, I nev - er been to heav -
- en, I did - n't know what it was like, but
E♭
3fr
God let me have a glimpse in my dream last night.
A♭
4fr
And I could {see you smil - in', / hear you laugh - in',} you were

Fm7
Eb
3fr
look - in' right at me. And for the first time in a long
time on your face I saw some peace.
And I knew
And I knew
Fm7
Eb/G
3fr
Ab
4fr
ev - 'ry - thing was gon - na be al - right
ev - 'ry - thing was gon - na be al - right.
1
Bb
Eb
3fr
Ab
4fr
on the oth - er side,

E♭
3fr
A♭
4fr
on the oth - er side.
E♭/G
3fr
Fm9
2
On the No more tears and
E♭/G
3fr
A♭
4fr
B♭
no more sad good - byes on the
E♭
3fr
A♭
4fr
oth - er side, on the

E♭
3fr
A♭sus2
3fr
A♭
4fr
oth - er side,
on the
E♭
3fr
A♭
4fr
oth - er side.
(The oth - er side.)
E♭
3fr
A♭
4fr
I'll see you on
N.C.
A♭
4fr
E♭
3fr
A♭maj9
3fr
the oth - er side.

OUR GOD IS IN CONTROL

Words and Music by STEVEN CURTIS CHAPMAN
and MARY BETH CHAPMAN

Moderate Ballad
Dm
C
B♭
F/A
Gm7
mp
1
2
F
This is not how it should be,
not where we planned to be
B♭
this is not how it could be,
when we start - ed this jour - ney,
Dm
but this is how it is,
but this is where we are,

C
F
Fsus
F
B♭sus2
and our God is in con - trol.
and our God is in con - trol.
This is
Though this
F
B♭
not how it will be
first taste is bit - ter,
when we fi - nal - ly will see,
there will be sweet - ness for - ev - er,
Dm
C
we'll see with our own eyes
when we fi - n'lly taste and see
He was al - ways in
that our God is in
F
Fsus
F
F/A
B♭maj7
con - trol.
con - trol.
And we'll sing, "Ho - ly,

C
Dm
Ho - ly, Ho - ly is our God," and we will
Bbmaj7
C
Dm
fi - n'lly real - ly un - der - stand what it means. So we'll sing,
Bbmaj7
C
Dm
"Ho - ly, Ho - ly, Ho - ly is our God,"
Gm7
1
Bbmaj9
5fr
while we're wait - ing for that day. This is

2
F/A
B♭
We're wait - ing for that day,
C
Dm
C
we'll keep on wait - ing for that day when we will
Gm7
Dm
C
know our God is in con - trol.
(Ho - ly,
B♭
F/A
Gm7
Ho - ly, Ho - ly.

Dm
C
B♭
F/A
Gm7
Ho - ly, Ho - ly, Ho - ly.)
Dm
C
B♭
F/A
Our God is in con - trol.
(Ho - ly, Ho - ly,
Gm7
Dm
C
Our God is in con - trol.
Ho - ly. Ho - ly,
B♭
F/A
Gm7
Ho - ly, Ho - ly.)

SAFELY HOME

Words and Music by
JON MOHR

Gently, somewhat freely
N.C.
mp
E
B
B/A
E
B/D♯
C♯m7
B/D♯
E
B/D♯
C♯m7
B/D♯
E
B/D♯
C♯m7
B/D♯
E
B/D♯
C♯m7
B
Chil - dren, pre - cious chil - dren, I know you're
hear Me. Come, draw near Me. Their pain is
A
E/G♯
A
B
A
E/G♯
1
A
B
shak - en, a loved one tak - en. Oh, but
passed now. They rest at last now,

2
A
B
E
B/D♯
C♯m7
B
𝄋
A
B/A
safe - ly home.
They are strong
Amaj7
E
A/E
E
A
B/A
and free.
They are safe
Amaj7
Bsus
B
E/B
B7
E
B/D♯
with Me.
This life
One day
rall.
a tempo
C♯m7
B/D♯
E
B/D♯
C♯m7
B
A
E/G♯
is near - ly shad - ow.
To - day there's sor - row,
you will join them,
all to - geth - er,

To Coda
A
B
A
E/G♯
A
B
E
B/D♯
4fr
but joy to - mor - row.
this time for - ev - er,
Safe - ly home.
D.S. al Coda
C♯m7
4fr
B
They are
CODA
A
B
E
B/D♯
4fr
C♯m7
4fr
B
safe - ly home.
A
E/G♯
A
B
E
B/D♯
4fr
Safe - ly home.
C♯m7
4fr
B
A(add2)
B(add2)
4fr
E
molto rit.

RAGING SEA

Words and Music by MICHAEL W. SMITH
and PAUL BALOCHE

Moderate Pop Ballad
B♭
E♭
3fr
Some-times the jour - ney makes you wea - ry,
mf

B♭
E♭
3fr
B♭/D
feels like a long and wind - ing road.

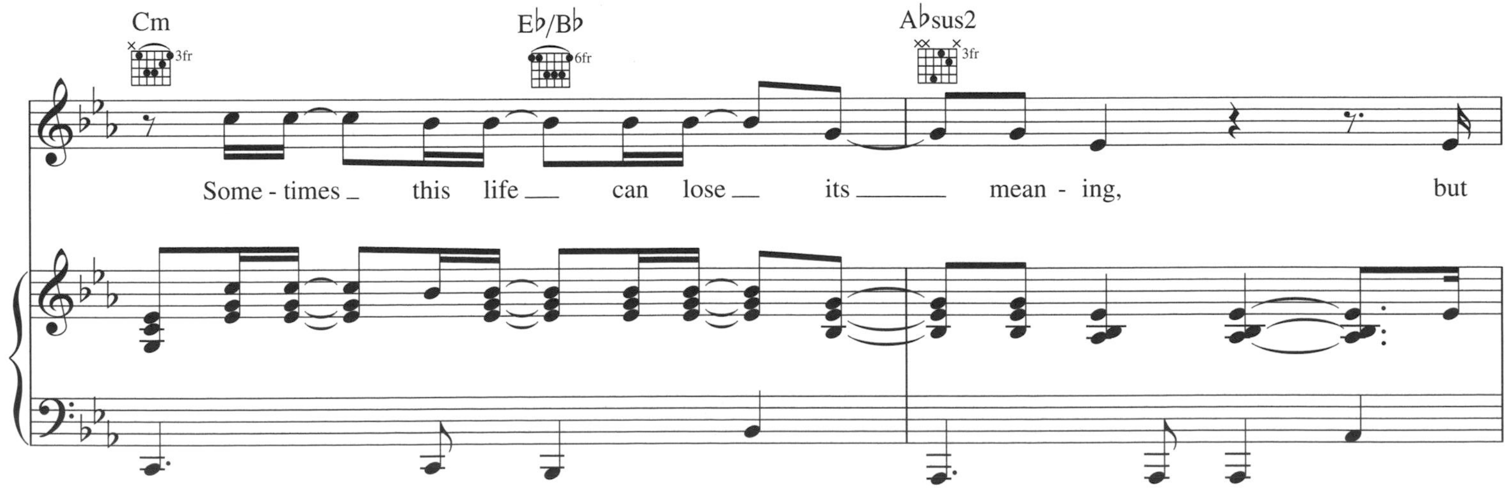
Cm
3fr
E♭/B♭
6fr
A♭sus2
3fr
Some-times this life can lose its mean - ing, but

Fm7(add4)
Eb/G
3fr
Bbsus
Bb
you might be surprised to find some hope.
Eb/Bb
6fr
Maybe you're wondering where love is.
Bb
Eb
3fr
Bb/D
You may feel it's far away from here.
Cm
3fr
Eb/Bb
6fr
Absus2
3fr
Maybe you're wondering where I am.

Fm7(add4)
Eb/G
3fr
Bbsus
Bb
You might be surprised to find I'm near.
Ab/Eb
Eb
3fr
Eb/G
3fr
And when your life is tossed and turning,
Ab
4fr
Bb
Cm
3fr
and you are on the rag - ing sea,
Eb/Bb
6fr
Csus
3fr
Cm
3fr
Cm/Bb
8fr
I'll come and pull you from the wa - ter.

To Coda
A♭
Fm7
B♭
E♭
Then you will know that you are free.
Cm
Cm7
B♭
So, if you're stum - bling through the val -
E♭/B♭
B♭
- ley,
if you're tempt - ed to give up the fight,
E♭
B♭/D
Cm
E♭/B♭
reach out your hand, and I will lead

A♭sus2
Fm7(add4)
E♭/G
you.
I will be your strong arm in the
B♭sus
B♭
D.S. al Coda
CODA
E♭
night.
free.
A♭/E♭
E♭
E♭/G
And when your life is tossed and turning,
A♭
B♭
Cm
and you are on the raging sea,

Eb/Bb
6fr
Csus
3fr
Cm
3fr
Cm/Bb
8fr
I'll come and pull you from the wa - ter.
Ab
4fr
Fm7
Bb
Eb/Bb
6fr
Then you will know that you are free.
Csus
3fr
Cm
3fr
Cm/Bb
8fr
I'll come and pull you from the wa - ter.
Ab
4fr
Fm7
Bb
Eb
3fr
Then you will know that you are free.
molto rit.

THERE WILL BE A DAY

Words and Music by
JEREMY CAMP

Moderate Ballad
Em7
Csus2
3fr
G/B
D/F♯
mp
Em7
Csus2
3fr
G/B
D/F♯
Em7
C
G
D
I try to hold on to this world with ev - 'ry - thing I have,
Em7
C
G/B
D/F♯
but I feel the weight of what it brings and the hurt that tries to grab.

* Recorded a half step lower.

Em7
C
G
D
The man-y trials that seem to nev-er end, His Word de-clares this truth,
Em7
C
G/B
D/F♯
that we will en-ter in His rest with won-ders a-new.
C
G/B
D
G/B
But I hold on to this hope and the prom-ise that He brings,
C
G/B
D
that there will be a place with no more suf-fer-ing. There will be a day

C
Em7
D
with no more tears, no more pain and no more fears.
G
C
There will be a day when the burdens of this place
Em7
D
G
will be no more; we'll see Jesus face to face. But un-
Em7
D/F♯
C
Em9
til that day, we'll hold on to You always.
mf

Cmaj9#11
Gmaj7
Gmaj7/D
Em7
C
I know the jour - ney seems so long,
G
D
Em7
C
you feel you're walk - ing on your own. But there has nev - er been a step
G/B
D/F#
Em7
C
where you've walked out all a - lone. Trou-bled soul, don't lose your heart,

G
D
Em7
C
'cause joy and peace He brings. And the beau - ty that's in store
G/B
D/F♯
C
G/B
out-weighs the hurt of life's sting. But I hold on to this hope
D
G/B
C
G/B
and the prom-ise that He brings. There will be a place with no
D
C
more suf-fer-ing. There will be a day with no more tears,
cresc.
f

Em7
D
G
G/B
no more pain and no more fears. There will be a day
C
Em7
when the bur-dens of this place will be no more;
D
G
we'll see Je-sus face to face. But un-til
Em
D/F♯
C
G/B
Am7
G
C
D
that day, we'll hold on to You al-ways.

Em
C/E
I can't wait _ un - til _ that day _ where the ver - y One _ I've lived _ for al - ways _ will
G/D
D
wipe a - way _ the sor - row that _ I've faced. _ Oh, to
Em
C/E
touch the scars _ that res - cued me _ from a life of shame _ and mis - er - y, oh,
G/D
D
C
this is why, _ this is why _ I sing. _ There will be a day _ with no more _ tears, _
mp

Em
D
G
no more pain and no more fears. There will be a day
C
Em
when the burdens of this place will be no more;
D
we'll see Jesus face to face. There will be a day
Em
C
G
with no more tears, no more pain and no more fears.
f

D
Em
C
There will be a day when the bur-dens of this place will be no more;
G
D
we'll see Je-sus face to face. There will be a day.
Em
C
He will wipe a-way the tears, He will wipe a-way the tears,
G
D
C
He will wipe a-way the tears. There will be a day.

SAVE A PLACE FOR ME

Words and Music by SAM MIZELL
and MATTHEW WEST

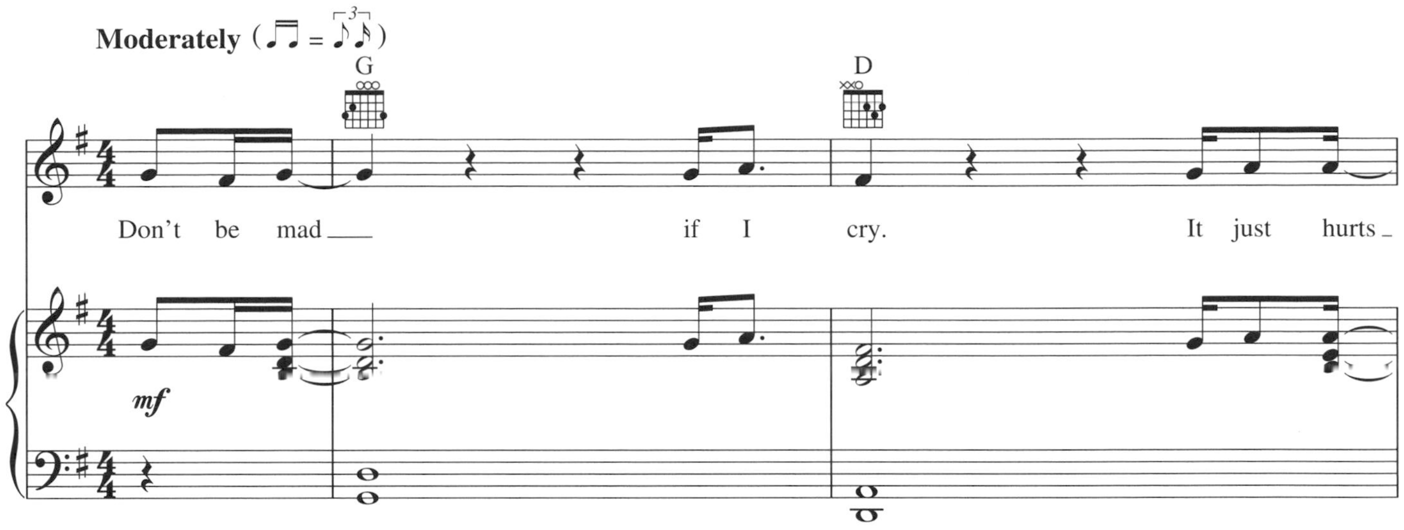
Moderately
G
D
Don't be mad
if I
cry.
It just hurts
mf

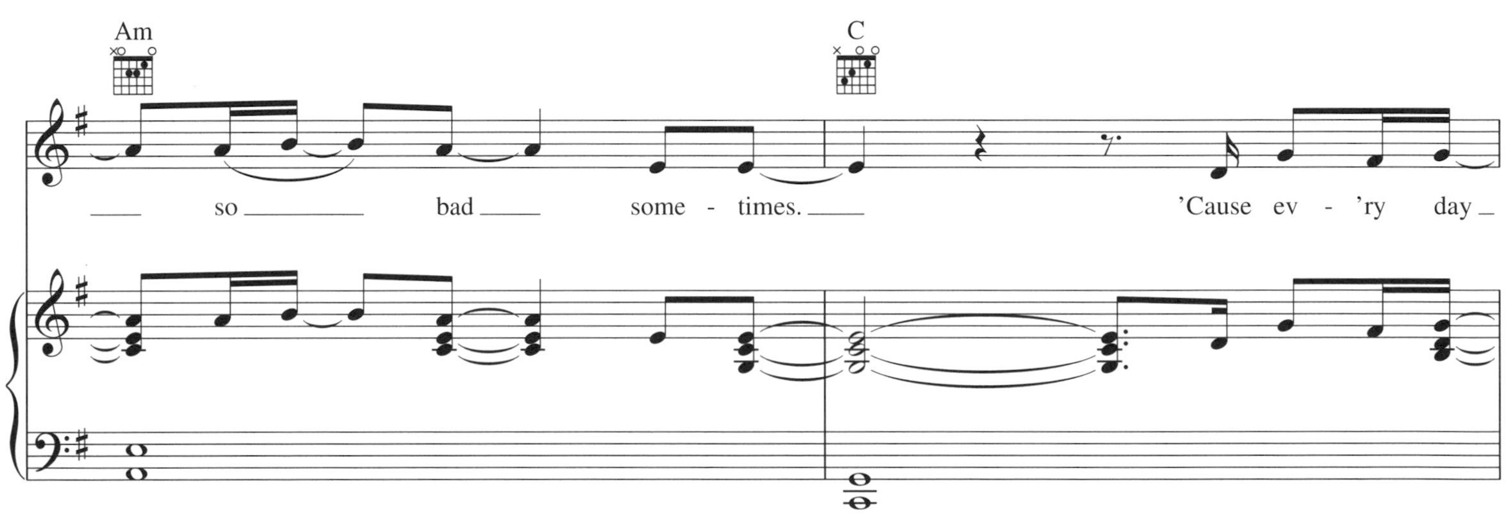
Am
C
so
bad
some - times.
'Cause ev - 'ry day

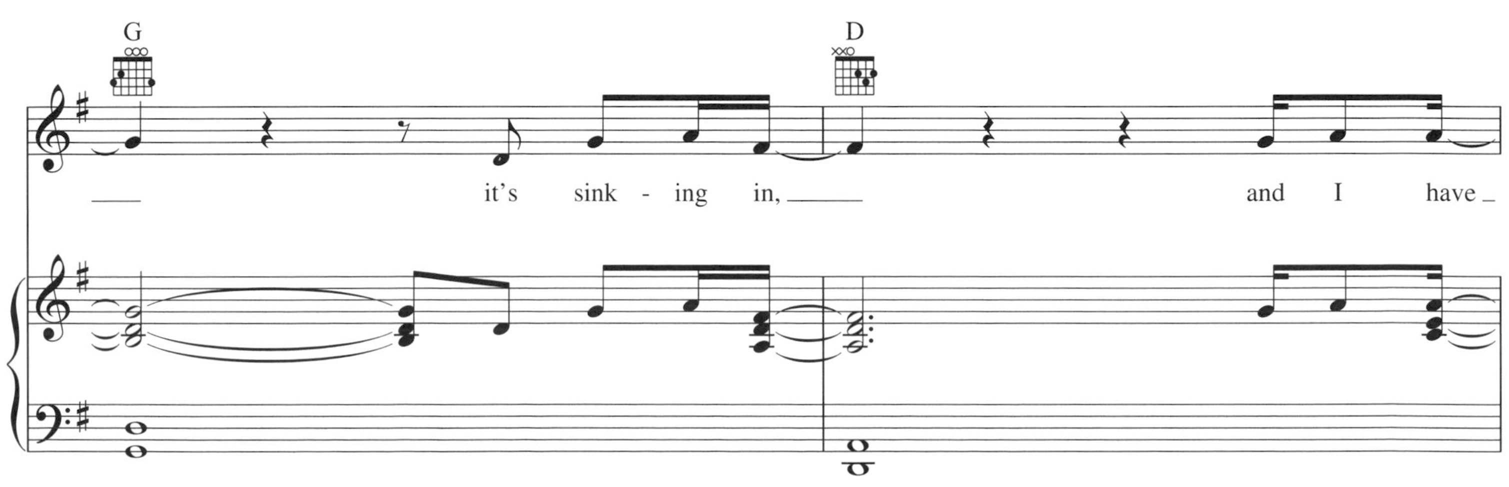
G
D
it's sink - ing in,
and I have

Am
C
to say good-bye all o - ver a - gain.
You know, I
D
Em
C
bet it feels good to have the weight of this world off your shoul - ders now.
I'm
D
Em
Csus2
3fr
dream-ing of the day when I'm fi - nal - ly there with you.
G
D
Save a place for me,
save a place for me,
save a place for me.

Am
C
I'll be there soon, I'll be there soon.
G
D
Save a place for me, save some grace for me.
To Coda
Am
C
Fsus2
I'll be there soon, I'll be there soon.
G
D
La da da, la da da. La da da da da da da.

Am
C
G
I have asked the ques - tions
D
Am
why, but I guess the an - swer's for an - oth - er time.
C
G
So in - stead, I'll pray with ev - 'ry
D
Am
tear, and be thank - ful for the time I had you

C
D.S. al Coda
CODA
C
here. So you just
I'll be there.
D
Em
Csus2
3fr
I wan-na live my life just like you did,
D
Em
Csus2
Csus2(♯4)
Csus2
and make the most of my time just like you did. And I wan-na make
D
Em
Csus2
my home up in the sky, just like you did. Oh,

but un - til I get there, un - til I get there, just
G
D
save a place for me, save a place for me,
Am9
5fr
C
N.C.
G
'cause I will be there soon.
D
Am7
G/B
Csus2
3fr

G
D
Save a place for me,
save a place for me.
Am
C
Fsus2
I'll be there soon,
I'll be there soon.
G
D
La da da,
la da da.
La da da
da da
da da.
Am
C
Fsus2
G
La da da,
la da da.
La da da
da da
da
da.

VISITOR FROM HEAVEN

Words and Music by
TWILA PARIS

E♭/G
A♭(add2)
gift of love to be re - turned.
We
E♭/G
A♭
A♭(add2)
think of you and smile.
A
A♭
B♭7
E♭
vis - i - tor from heav - en,
ac -
E♭/G
A♭maj7
B♭sus
B♭/D
com - pa - nied by grace,
re -

E♭/G
A♭
mind - ing of a bet - ter love, and
E♭/G
A♭
of a bet - ter place. With
B♭/D
E♭/G
A♭sus2
B♭sus
B♭/D
ach - ing hearts and emp - ty arms,
break - ing hearts and o - pen hands,
we
E♭/G
A♭(add2)
send you with a name. It

B♭/D
E♭/G
A♭sus2
B♭sus
B♭/D
E♭/G
hurts so much to let you go, but we're so glad you
To Coda
A♭(add2)
A♭maj7
B♭
came. We're so glad you
E♭
E♭/G
A♭maj7
B♭
E♭
came.
E♭/G
A♭maj7
B♭
E♭
E♭maj7/B♭
A♭(add2)
E♭/G

Fm7(add4)
Ebmaj7/G
Ab(add2)
4fr
3
Ebmaj7/G
Ab(add2)
4fr
Bb7sus
Bb
A
3
Eb/G
3fr
Abmaj7
Bb7
Eb
3fr
vis - i - tor from heav - en, if
Eb/G
3fr
Abmaj7
Bbsus
Bb
on - ly for a day. We

Eb/G
3fr
Ab
4fr
thank Him for the time He gave, and
now it's time to say:
We
Bb/D
Bbsus
trust you to the Fa - ther's love and
to His ten - der care,
3
and

Bb
Eb/G
Ab
Bbsus
Bb
in the ev - er-last - ing arms,
and
Eb/G
Ab
we're so glad you're there.
Eb/G
Ab(add2)
Bb/Ab
Ab(add2)
D.S. al Coda
We're so glad you're there.
With
CODA
Abmaj7
Bb
Eb
Eb/G
We're so glad you came.

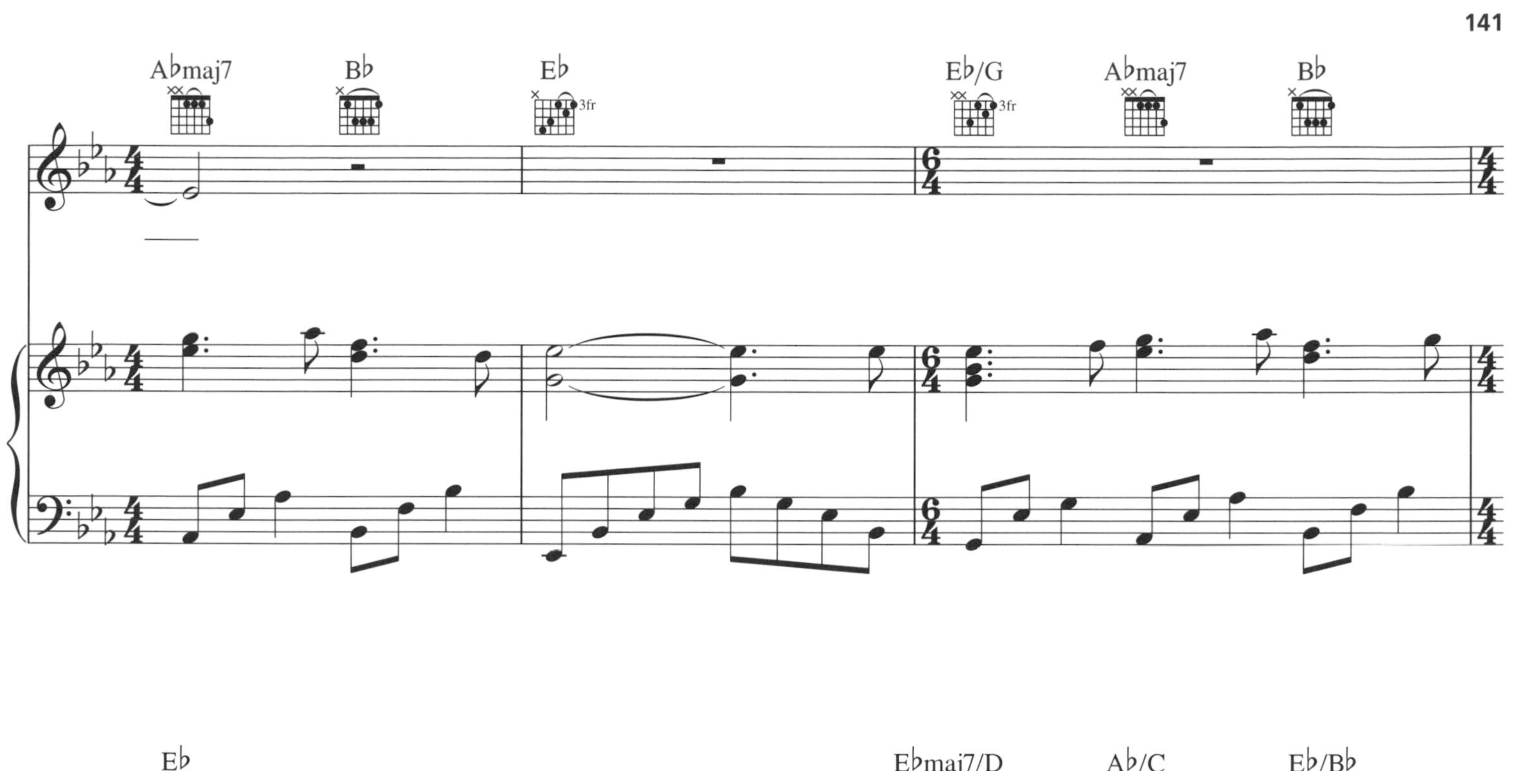
A♭maj7
B♭
E♭
3fr
E♭/G
3fr
A♭maj7
B♭

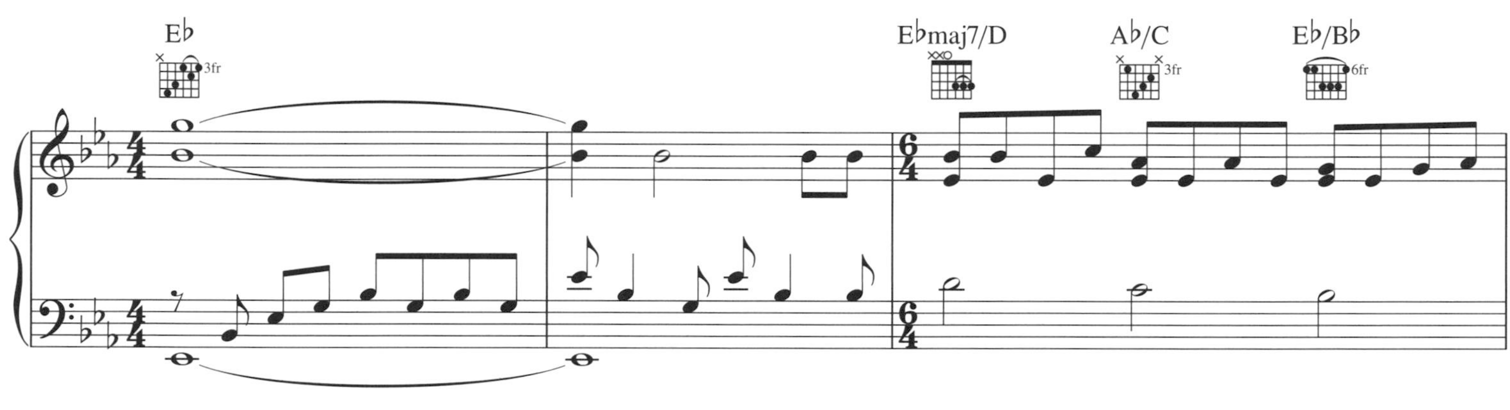
E♭
3fr
E♭maj7/D
A♭/C
3fr
E♭/B♭
6fr

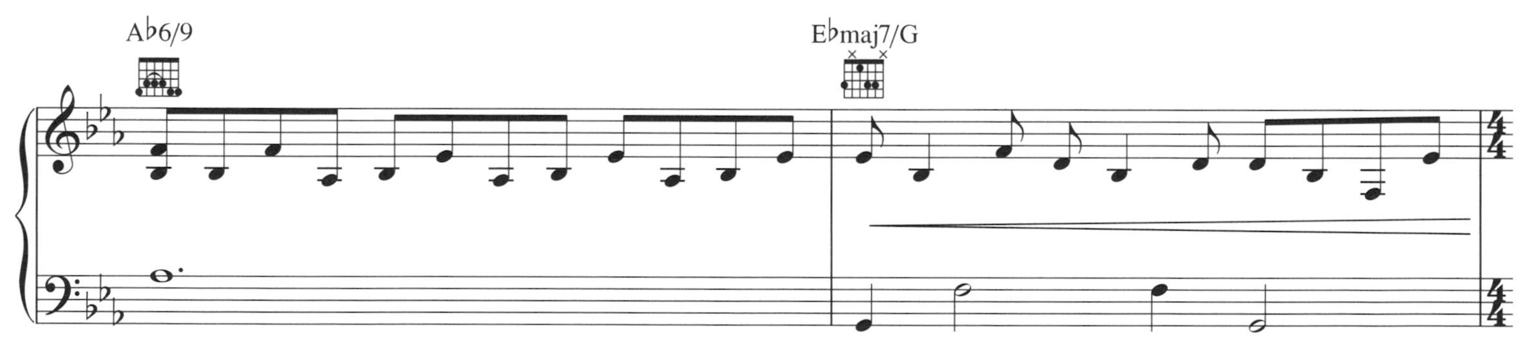
A♭6/9
E♭maj7/G

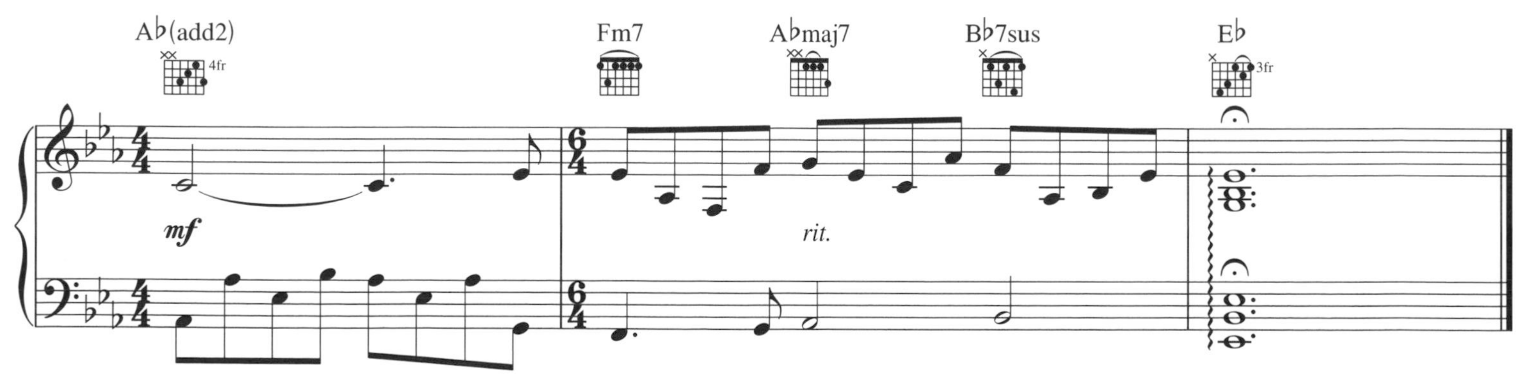
A♭(add2)
4fr
Fm7
A♭maj7
B♭7sus
E♭
3fr
mf
rit.

WHEN ANSWERS AREN'T ENOUGH

Words and Music by SCOTT WESLEY BROWN
and GREG NELSON

Moderately
A/E
B9/E
Bm7/E
E/D
C♯m7
4fr
F♯m7
mf
Dmaj7
D6
Dmaj7/E
E7
A(add2)
A
D/A
A
E/G♯
You have faced the moun - tains ___ of des - per - a - tion. You have
F♯m7
C♯m/E
4fr
B/D♯
4fr
climbed, you have fought, you have won. But this

D E/D C♯m7 F♯m Bm7 A/C♯
val - ley that lies cold - ly be - fore you casts a shad - ow you can - not o - ver -
A/D Bm/D F♯m/E E A D/A
come. And just when you thought you had it all to -
A E/G♯ F♯m7 C♯m/E B/D♯
geth - er, you knew ev - 'ry verse to get you through. But
D E/D C♯m7 F♯m7
this time all the sor - row broke more than just your heart, and re -

Bm7
A/C♯
D/E
E
cit - ing all those vers - es just won't do. When
A
A/C♯
A/D
Bm/D
an - swers aren't e - nough, there is Je - sus. He is
A/E
D♯m7♭5
6fr
D/E
E
more than just an an - swer to your prayer, and your
F♯m
A/C♯
D
Bm7
To Coda
heart will find a safe and peace - ful ref - uge. When

A/E
Bm7/E
E
A
Dmaj9
D6
4fr
an - swers aren't e - nough, He is there.
F♯m/E
E
A
D/A
A
E/G♯
In - stead of ask - ing why did it hap - pen, think of
F♯m7
C♯m/E
4fr
B/D♯
4fr
3
where it can lead you from here. And as your
D
E/D
C♯m7
4fr
F♯m7
pain is slow - ly eas - ing, you can find a great - er rea - son to

Bm7
A/C♯
Bm7/E
E
D.S. al Coda
live your life tri - um - phant through the tears. When
CODA
A/E
Bm7/E
E
F
E♭/F
F
an - swers aren't e - nough, He is there. When
cresc.
rall.
B♭
B♭/D
B♭/E♭
Cm/E♭
3fr
an - swers aren't e - nough, there is Je - sus. He is
f a tempo
B♭/F
Em7♭5
E♭/F
F
more than just an an - swer to your prayer, and your

Gm
B♭/D
E♭
Cm7
heart will find a safe and peace - ful ref - uge. When
B♭/F
Cm7/F
F♯dim7
Gm
Gm7/C
C7
B♭/F
Edim/F
an - swers aren't e - nough, He is there. When an - swers aren't e -
dim.
mf
F7sus
F7
E♭maj7
F/E♭
E♭maj7
nough, He is there.
B♭sus2/D
Gm7
Cm7
E♭/F
F7
B♭
rit.

WHEN IT'S ALL BEEN SAID AND DONE

Words and Music by
JAMES A. COWAN

F
C
Am
Em
just one thing that mat - ters.
treas - ures will mean noth - ing.
Did I
On - ly
F
C
Em7
Am
F
Gsus
3fr
G
do my best to live for truth, did I live my life for You?
what I've done for love's re - ward will stand the test of time.
1
C
When it's
2
C
F
C
G
Am
F
G
C
Lord, Your

F
C
G
Am
Em7
mer - cy is so great
that You
al - ways sing Your praise
here on
F
C
Am
Em
look be - yond our weak - ness
and find
earth and ev - er af - ter,
for You've
F
C
Em7
Am
1
F
Gsus
G
3fr
pur - est gold in mir - y clay,
mak-ing sin-ners in - to saints.
shown me heav - en's my true home
when it's
C
C/E
2
F
Gsus
G
Am
G6
Fmaj7
C/E
3fr
I will
all been said and done.
You're my

Dm7
Gsus
3fr
G
C
F
C
life when life is gone.
G
Am
F
Gsus
3fr
G
C
When it's
F
C
G
Am
Em
all been said and done
there is
F
C
Am
Em
just one thing that mat - ters.
Did I

F C Em7 Am
do my best to live for truth, did I
F Gsus G Am G Fmaj7 C/E
live my life for You? Lord, I
Dm7 Gsus G C F C
live my life for You.
G Am F Gsus G7 C
rit.

WITH HOPE

Words and Music by
STEVEN CURTIS CHAPMAN

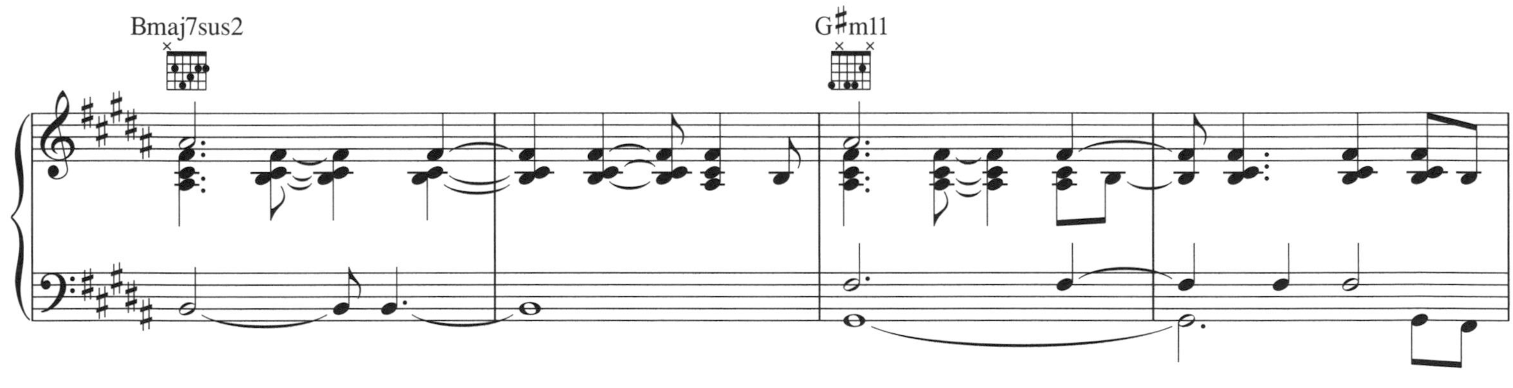

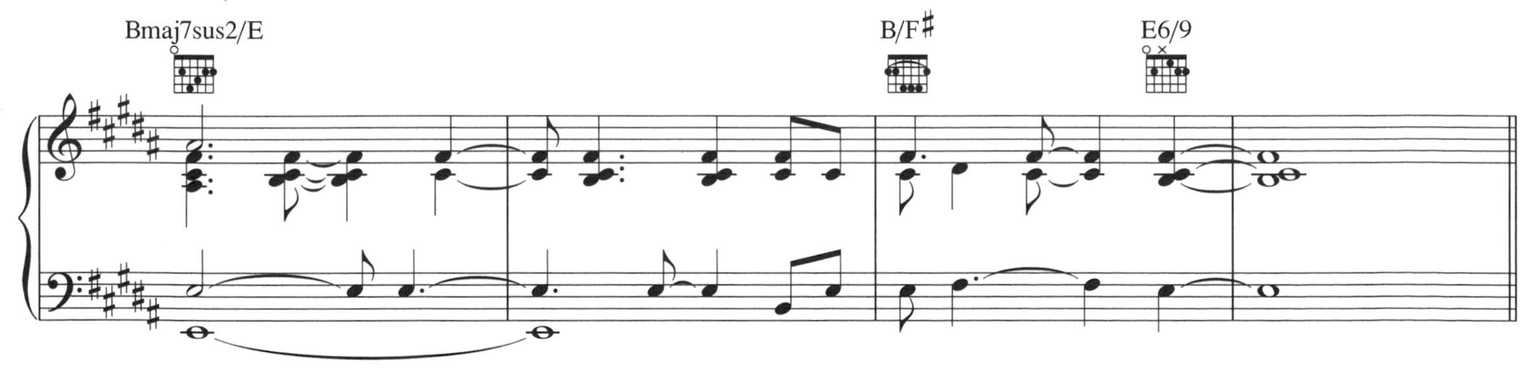

F#(add4)
E6/9
D#m7
C#m11
This is not at all how we thought it was
nev - er have I known an - y - thing so hard
Bsus2
Bsus2/A#
sup - posed to be. We had so man - y plans
to un - der - stand, and nev - er have I ques -
G#m11
E6/9
for you; we had so man - y dreams, and
- tioned more the wis - dom of God's plan. But
F#(add4)
E6/9
Bmaj7(add2)/D#
C#m7b5
now you've gone a - way and left us with our mem -
through the cloud of tears I see the Fa - ther smile

B(add2)
Bsus2/A♯
- 'ries of ___ your smile. ___ And noth - ing we ___ can say ___
___ and say, ___ "Well done." ___ And I i - mag - ine you ___
G♯m11
E6/9
___ and noth - ing we ___ can do ___ can take a -
___ where you want - ed most ___ to be, ___ see - ing
F♯/E
E6/9
F♯/E
E6/9
- way ___ the pain, the pain of los - ing you. ___
all your dreams ___ come true, ___ 'cause now you're home and now ___ you're free. ___
F♯/B
B(add2)
When
And
we can cry ___ with hope, ___ we can

F♯/G♯
G♯m11
E6/9
Em(maj7)
say good - bye with hope, 'cause we know our good - bye
B(add2)
F♯sus
F♯(add4)
is not the end, oh no. And
F♯/B
B(add2)
F♯/G♯
G♯m11
we can grieve with hope, 'cause we be - lieve with hope
To Coda
E6
Em(maj7)
there's a place where we'll see your face a - gain.

1
F♯/B
B(add9)
7fr
F♯/G♯
G♯m
4fr
G♯m/F♯
4fr
We'll see your
F♯/E
E6/9
F♯sus
E6/9
face a - gain.
And
2
A(add2)
B(add2)
4fr
We'll see your
A(add2)
B(add2)
4fr
face a - gain,
yeah.
We'll see your

A(add2)
G♯m7
4fr
face a - gain.
And we have this hope
pp
B(add2)/F♯
C♯m
4fr
E(add2)/B
as an an - chor,
'cause we be - lieve
that ev - 'ry - thing
God
Amaj7
D.S. al Coda
prom - ised us is true.
So
rit.
a tempo
CODA
E6/9
place...
Em6
B(add2)/D♯
4fr
C♯
E6/9
by God's grace,
there's a place
where we'll

A9
5fr
Bmaj7sus2
see your face again.
rit.
a tempo
G♯m11
Bmaj7sus2/E
3
We'll see your face a-gain.
F♯/E
So
F♯/B
B(add2)
4fr
F♯/A♯
4fr
F♯/G♯
G♯m11
we can cry with hope

F♯/E
E6/9
and say good - bye with hope.
F♯
E6/9
F♯/E
E6/9
F♯
E6/9
1, 2
We wait with hope
and we ache with hope.
Instrumental
3
F♯/E
E6/9
End instrumental We hold on with hope.

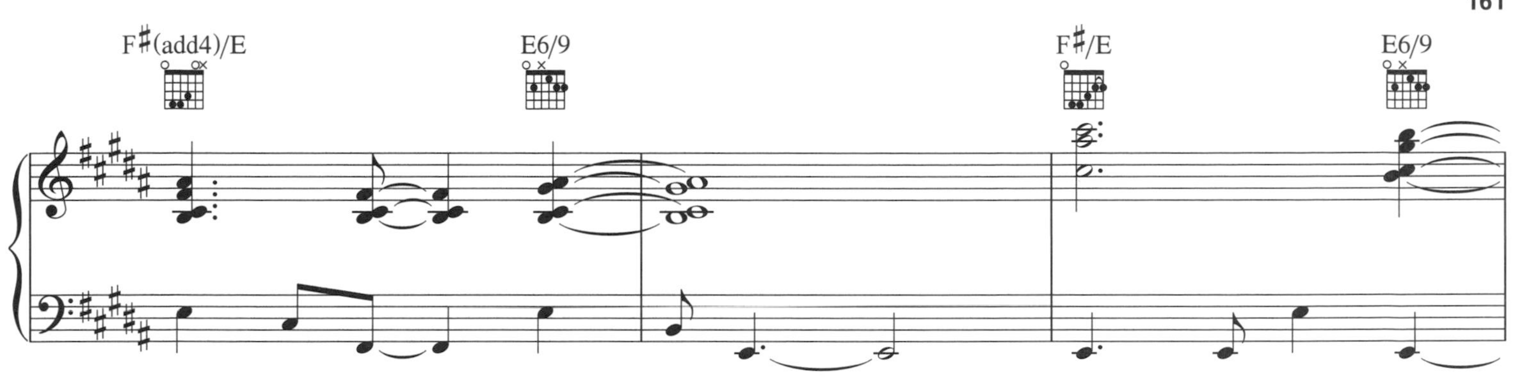
F♯(add4)/E
E6/9
F♯/E
E6/9

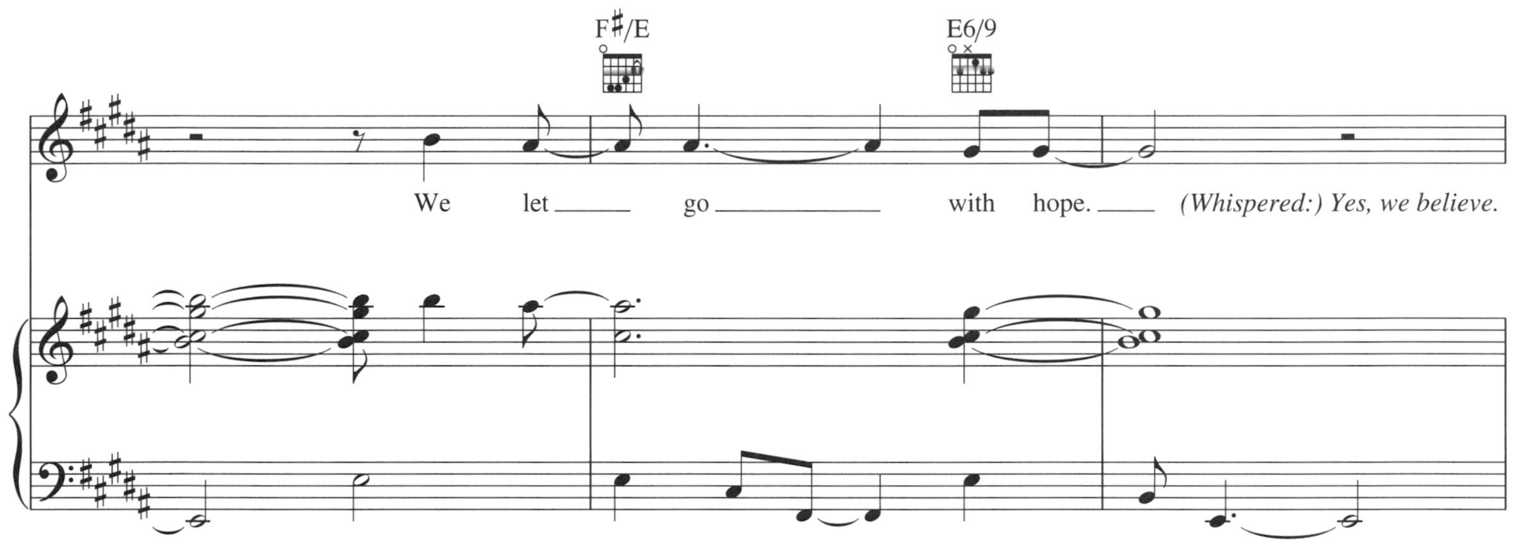
F♯/E
E6/9
We let go with hope. (Whispered:) Yes, we believe.

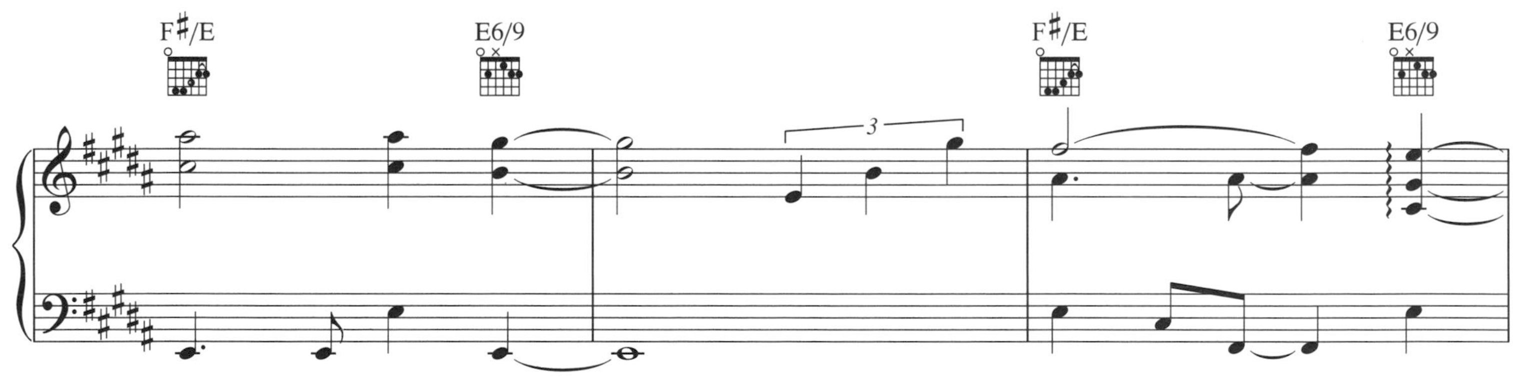
F♯/E
E6/9
F♯/E
E6/9
3

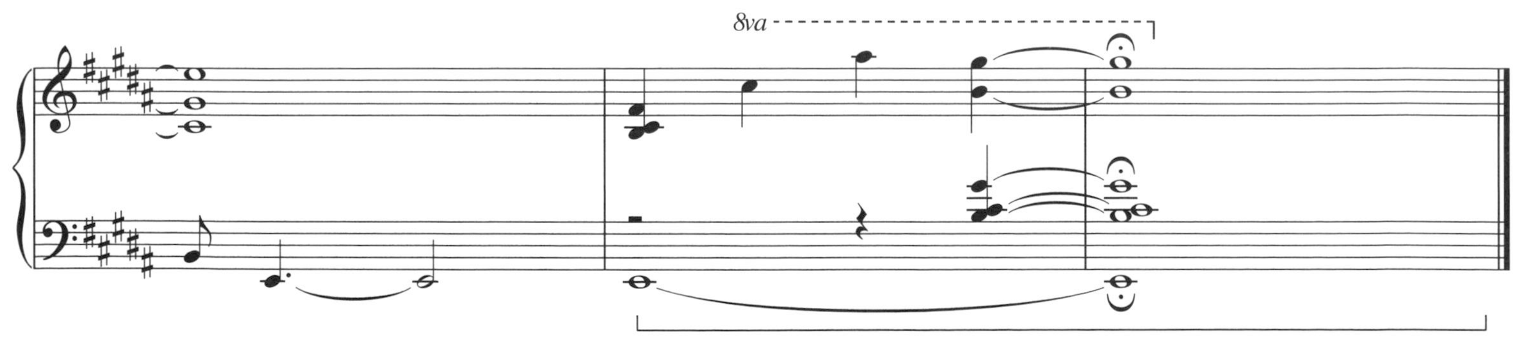
8va

WISH YOU WERE HERE

Words and Music by PETE KIPLEY
and DAN MUCKALA

Slowly, in 2
D
D/C#
D/C
mp
G6/9/B
D
D/C#
I want - ed to tell _ you how close - ly I've kept the
D/C
G/B
D
mem - 'ries of you _ in my heart. And all of the life - times _ that
A/C#
D/C
G/B
we've had to share _ live e - ven though _ we're a - part. _

G
A/G
D(add2)/F♯
D/F♯
But don't cry for me,
'cause I'm fi - nal - ly
Em(add2)
Em
free
to run with the an - gels on
D
streets made of gold,
to lis - ten to sto - ries of saints, new and old,
to
A/C♯
wor - ship our Mak - er.
That's where I'll be
when you fi - n'lly
To Coda

Gm(maj7)
3fr
G6
D
D/C♯
find me.
D/C
G6/9/B
Gsus2/B
D
Now, don't you be wea - ry, 'cause
mf
A/C♯
D/C
G/B
wait-ing for you are won-ders that you've nev - er known. Just
D
A/C♯
D/C
hold on to Je - sus, reach out for His hand, and one day they'll wel-come you

G/B
G
A/G
D(add2)/F♯
D/F♯
home.
And that's when you'll be
G
A/G
Em(add2)
Em
D.S. al Coda
fi - nal - ly free,
fi - nal - ly free to
CODA
Gm(maj7)
Gm6
3fr
Asus
A7
C(add2)
find me.
I wish you were here.
f
G(add2)/B
C(add2)
G(add2)/B
I wish you were here.
And all of the dreams

C(add2)
G/B
Gm/B♭
that you treas - ure will soon come to-geth - er, and that's when your sor - row
Asus
A7
N.C.
will find to-mor - row, and you will rise a - gain to
A
E
A
run with the an - gels on streets made of gold, to lis-ten to sto - ries of
E
B/D♯
A
E
B/D♯
saints, new and old, to wor-ship our Mak - er. That's where you'll be

1
2
A
B/E
E
when you fi - n'lly find me. We'll
when you fi - n'lly
Am(maj7)
Am6
Bsus
find me.
I wish you were here.
dim.
mp
E(add2)/G#
E/G#
4fr
I wish you were here.
Gmaj7
G6
D(add2)/F#
D/F#
G(add2)

YOU WOULDN'T CRY
(Andrew's Song)

Words and Music by MANDISA HUNDLEY,
CATT GRAVITT and CINDY MORGAN

Moderately fast
D
Bm
*
All you saw was pain,
p

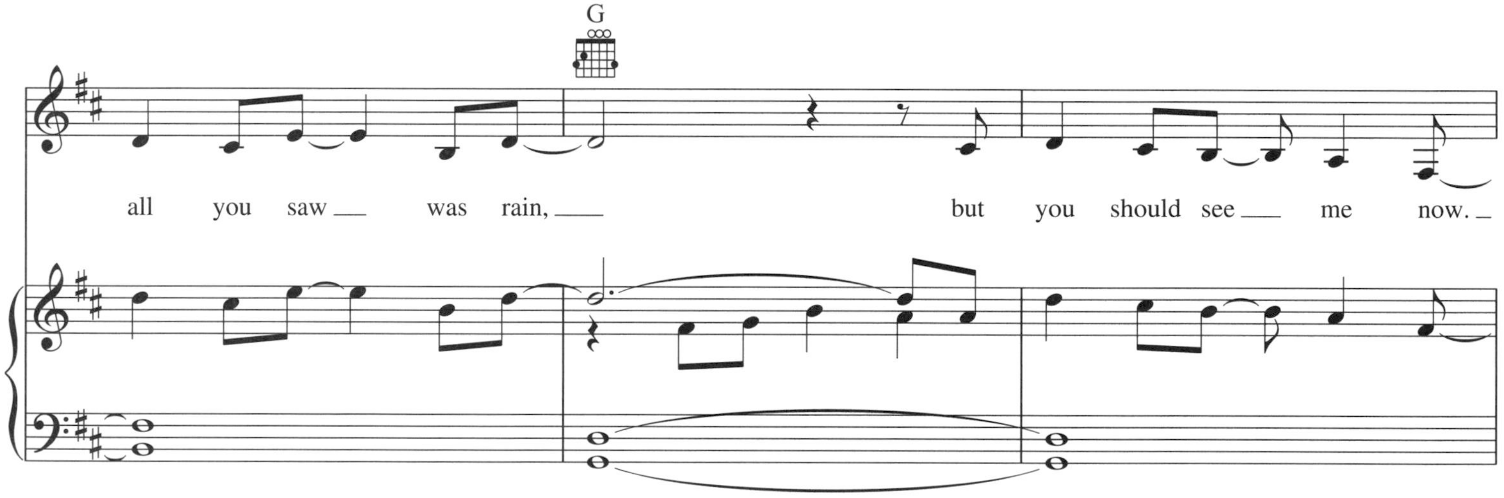
G
all you saw was rain,
but you should see me now.

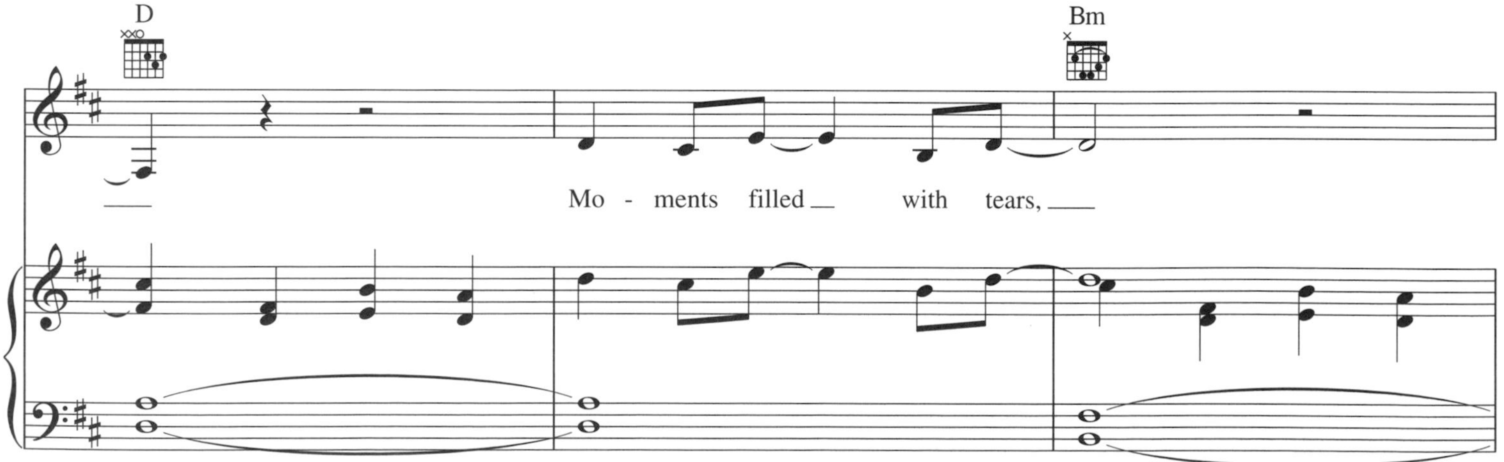
D
Bm
Mo - ments filled with tears,

* Recorded a half step lower.

G
last - ed all those years,
dis - ap - peared some - how.
D
Em7
D/F♯
You nev - er said good - bye,
on your knees you cry.
mp
G
Asus
D
You're still ask - ing why.
But blue has nev - er been blu -
mf
Dsus2/F♯
Gsus2
Bm7
A
- er, true has nev - er been tru - er.
Hon -

D
D/F♯
- ey nev - er tast - ed so sweet. There's a song in the breeze,
Gsus2
Bm7
A
D
a mil - lion voic - es in praise. A rose has nev - er smelled red -
Dsus2/F♯
Gsus2
Bm7
A
- der, the sun has nev - er been bright - er. If I
D
D/F♯
could find the right words to say, if you could look at my face,

To Coda
Gsus2
Bm
A
if you could just see this place, you would-n't cry for me
D
Bm7
to-day. What you think you see
Gsus2
is-n't real-ly me. I'm al-read-y home.
D
Bm7
You've got to lay it down, 'cause

Gsus2
Je - sus holds me now, and I am not a - lone.
D
Em7
D/F#
Your faith is wear - ing thin, but I am watch - ing Him,
Gsus2
Asus
D.S. al Coda
and He is hold - ing You, too. And
CODA
Bm
A
Csus2
3fr
you would - n't cry for me to - day,
f

G
D
you would-n't cry for me to-day.
Csus2
Oh, what may seem like years
G/B
A7sus
N.C.
D
will just be a mo - ment.
Oh, the day
Csus2
G/B
will come when I'll show you where you're go -

Asus
A
- ing. I can't wait to show you that blue
D
D(add2)/F♯
Gsus2
has nev - er been blu - er, true has nev - er been tru -
mp sub.
Bm
A
D
D/F♯
er. Hon - ey nev - er tast - ed so sweet. There's a song in the breeze,
Gsus2
Bm7
A
a mil - lion voic - es in praise. A rose
cresc.

D
Dsus2/F♯
has nev - er smelled red - der, the sun
f
Gsus2
Bm7
A
has nev - er been bright - er. If I
D
D/F♯
could find the right words to say, if you could look at my face,
Gsus2
Bm
A
if you could just see this place, you would - n't cry for me

Csus2
3fr
G
D
to - day,
you would-n't cry for me to - day.
Dsus2/F♯
G(add2)
D
Dsus2/F♯
You would-n't cry for me to - day, you would - n't cry
Gsus2
Bm
Asus
for me to - day, would-n't cry for me to - day.